DODGING THE BULLET
An Inside Washington Look At High-Stakes Lobbying Against an Oil Giant

EDWARD L. JAFFEE

AuthorHouse™
1663 Liberty Drive
Bloomington, IN 47403
www.authorhouse.com
Phone: 1-800-839-8640

© 2011 Edward L. Jaffee. All rights reserved.

No part of this book may be reproduced, stored in a retrieval system, or transmitted by any means without the written permission of the author.

First published by AuthorHouse 2/10/2011

ISBN: 978-1-4567-0064-5 (dj)
ISBN: 978-1-4567-0066-9 (e)
ISBN: 978-1-4567-0065-2 (sc)

Library of Congress Control Number: 2010917090

Printed in the United States of America

Any people depicted in stock imagery provided by Thinkstock are models, and such images are being used for illustrative purposes only. Certain stock imagery © Thinkstock.

This book is printed on acid-free paper.

Because of the dynamic nature of the Internet, any Web addresses or links contained in this book may have changed since publication and may no longer be valid. The views expressed in this work are solely those of the author and do not necessarily reflect the views of the publisher, and the publisher hereby disclaims any responsibility for them.

ACKNOWLEDGEMENTS

The files that form the backbone of this book sat on the floor in my home office for some twenty-five years until my wife Sharon finally prevailed on me to put the story down on paper. So clearly, the book is dedicated to her.

Beyond that, however, I am indebted to Bill Stover for his invaluable critiques along the way, and especially to George Vercessi for his continued encouragement and helpful advice throughout the project. And my deep thanks to Sky Phillips of the Northern Virginia Writers' Group for her constant early support, and to Fred Surls for his eagle-eyed proofreading.

And finally, the staff at the Library of Congress were both patient and kind in their assistance, as were a host of good friends who reviewed early chapters and offered helpful suggestions.

FOREWORD

This slim volume recounts the ups and downs of a major lobbying effort in 1983-'84 that involved several Fortune 500 companies doing extended battle with an oil industry giant, Texaco. The book aims to provide an interesting and enjoyable read, while giving the reader an inside look at how this kind of lobbying is usually done. For while the public constantly hears about high-priced lobbyists buying their way to power with payoffs, that really is the rare exception.

The overwhelming majority of cases, big or small, involve the nitty-gritty of carefully preparing arguments, making phone calls, office visits and just knowing how to interact with others.

As for the story itself, it is a personal memoir -- in part, almost a diary -- based largely on files retained for some 27 years. The names in the book are real. In a few cases I simply refer to the "staffer" or "legislative aide." The newspaper articles are verbatim, with some excisions to make for a smoother flow between article and story line.

The reader may find what seems to be a dizzying array of names to keep track of in the course of the story. They are included to provide an idea of the intricacies of day-to-day lobbying on Capitol Hill. That said, and in order to avoid constant, repeated references to the 42 members of the House Energy and Commerce Committee and the 22 on the Senate Energy and Natural Resources Committee in 1983-84, there is an appendix at the back of the book listing those members.

Just a quick reminder that at the time the events in this book took place, we were nowhere near as advanced as we are today in terms of communications. Fax machines were new, and there were no personal computers, cell phones, iPads or any of today's other communications shortcuts.

And -- unlike today -- 1983-'84 was also a time when congressmen and senators were willing to reach across the aisle to work on legislation. You have to wonder how things might be today if that were still true.

I have tried to recount the events of the story as accurately as possible. That said, any mistakes are solely mine.

Edward L. Jaffee
Springfield, Virginia
December 2010

CHAPTER ONE

"A KEY ISSUE FOR US"

MARCH 7, 1983 -- IT WAS a meeting pretty much like any other in my typical day as a Washington government affairs representative with PPG Industries: this one held by the Energy Committee of the National Association of Manufacturers, located on Pennsylvania Avenue in Washington. The long table in the main conference room was nearly full, with some 40 corporate government affairs reps, lobbyists who focused, at least in part, on energy issues. Energy was a secondary issue for me, with environmental matters as my main concern. But this meeting was to cover natural gas decontrol legislation, a subject that figured to significantly affect my employer.

Jim Rubin of Allied Chemical chaired the group, and the meeting. The session dragged on for more than three hours, as Rubin and others plodded through the entire 488-page Reagan administration proposed natural gas decontrol bill, called the Natural Gas Policy Act Amendments of 1983 and given the bill number S. 615 in the Senate. Each attendee was handed a copy. Attorney Gordon Gooch held forth for part of the time, with lucid explanations of what various sections of the bill meant to industrial users of natural gas. Not surprisingly, most in the room were pleased with what they were hearing. After all, it meant less government intervention in the marketplace.

Rob Odle, head of the Department of Energy's lobbying office, was also on hand, and emphasized the Reagan administration's strong support of the bill.

I was struck by the number of outside attorneys at the table, many of them sitting next to the Washington rep from their corporate clients. One of the best-known lawyers in the room, John Camp, was seated beside Don Annett, the vice president in charge of Texaco's Washington office.

After two hours, I was finding it increasingly difficult to keep my attention locked on the arcane discussion, and took a break to stretch in the anteroom just outside the conference room. I used the time to grab one of the three phones there and call Bob Steder, the go-to guy on energy within PPG's Supply Department. I had told him that morning that the meeting was on for today, and that I would get back to him if I saw anything that might be important to the company.

"So far, it's boring as hell," I offered. "But we'll see if anything develops."

"Well, get back in there and stay alert, Ed. This could be a key issue for us."

* * *

It was now past noon. The meeting had gone on since 9:30, and matters were winding down. Rubin was nearing the end of the proposed legislation, in Section 316, on page 414. As he read the section title: "First Sale, Direct Sale, Not-for-Resale Intrastate Gas," the light bulb came on in my head. *Direct sale, not-for-resale.* I knew, from spending several days at PPG's largest facility, at Lake Charles, Louisiana, that it purchased natural gas from Texaco, for use both as a fuel source and to break into its component parts, including ethane and ethylene. We used those components in making compounds called chemical intermediates to sell to other companies for use in manufacturing end-use products.

Given that PPG Lake Charles was the third largest industrial plant in the state, with well over 2,000 employees, I paid close attention as Rubin went through the brief section. Then, for the second time that morning, I slipped out to the anteroom, and found a phone in the corner. Steder had not yet gone to lunch.

"I think we may have something here," I told him. "Something that could be big."

"Shoot," was the reply. Bob Steder, a roly-poly outgoing type, was all business when it mattered.

I read the entire section over the phone, including the actuating words: "Any two parties to a first-sale, direct-sale, not-for-resale contract for intrastate natural gas will have until January 1, 1985, to renegotiate said contract to their mutual agreement. In the instance of failure to reach such an accord, either party may market out." I added that in checking the glossary of terms at the back of the bill, it turned out that *"market out"* meant to use the price for natural gas as of January 1, 1985.

Silence, for several seconds, and then, "Shit, man! This could *kill us* at Lake Charles!"

CHAPTER TWO

"A SWEET DEAL"

MARCH 7 -- BEFORE I could ask for specifics, Steder continued: "Our sole supplier of natural gas at Lake Charles is Texaco. There's a feeder line that goes directly from one of their main pipelines into our facility. That's why we're in a first-sale, direct sale situation. And since we use the gas right there, it's not for resale."

"Right," I interjected. "We use the gas as feedstock and as heating fuel."

"Yes, but it's the *amount* we use that's the key. Lake Charles chews up more than a hundred million cubic feet of gas every single day. That's enough to heat the whole city of Lake Charles twice over."

I exhaled, "Damn!"

"Now, from what you've just told me, Ed, this bill would cost us dearly. Back in 1967, when natural gas was so cheap that Texaco and other companies were actually flaring it off into the air, we signed a twenty-year contract with them to buy the stuff at 18 cents per mcf (*thousand cubic feet*). The deal expires on March 1, 1987, and includes a one-penny escalator every four years, so that as of today, we're paying them 22 cents per mcf."

I added the obvious: "Sounds like a sweet deal to me."

"It's what the contract calls for. But Texaco's ticked off because natural gas is now at about $2.80 cents per mcf. Remember what the Arab oil embargo did to the price of gasoline back in '73? Well, sometimes when you drill for oil, you first hit natural gas. Texaco did, and they were smart enough to tap into the gas as a huge cash cow. Hell, they were bragging, back in 1967, that they'd been able to entice major industry to locate in South Louisiana because of the available long-term supply of cheap natural gas. They said that in one of their annual reports."

"So, what happened when the '73 Arab oil embargo shot up the price of natural gas as well as gasoline?" I asked.

"Good question. Texaco immediately took us to court in Louisiana and tried to abrogate the contract. They claimed something called *force majeure*, an act of God. The court threw the case out, based on the doctrine of sanctity of contract, and added that an act of OPEC was not, in their mind, an act of God.

"Then," Steder continued, "Texaco tried and failed to break the contract by going to the state legislature. Their sponsor there at the time was a guy named Billy Tauzin, and I think you introduced me to him as a U.S. congressman last month in Washington."

"Right," I replied, struck by the irony. "What goes around, comes around."

"Whaddya mean?" Steder asked.

"Well, I'd assume Texaco will want to get Billy Tauzin to push the House version of this bill for them." The House bill, which I hadn't yet seen, was numbered HR-1517.

"Don't forget, Ed, that while Texaco is a bigger company than PPG, we're the larger player in Louisiana. And thousands of jobs could be at stake there."

"That may or may not matter," I countered. "Look, do we know who else, if anybody down there, has contracts like ours with Texaco? We're gonna need allies, Bob."

"Okay," came the answer. "Give me a few hours to run the traps and see, and also to try to figure out the dollar impact on PPG if this bill goes through."

"So," I concluded, "I assume that if this is as big as we think, I have your okay to do whatever is necessary to get that language out of the bill?"

"You really need to *ask*?"

CHAPTER THREE

"A MAJOR RAINMAKER"

MARCH 8 -- IT WAS the next morning at 9:30 before Steder called back.

"It's every bit as bad as I feared," he began. "The hit on PPG would be more than three hundred million dollars." (In today's numbers, that would have amounted to more than half a billion.) "That's based on a $2.80 per mcf price from January 1, 1985, until March 1, 1987, when the contract expires, and it includes some down time at the plant."

"Oy," I blurted.

"Oy indeed. And we're not alone in being at risk. I have no idea of the specifics, but Kaiser Aluminum and Chemical, plus Georgia Pacific and Air Products all have Louisiana facilities and they all have the same kind of contracts with Texaco, negotiated at varying times. And by the way, I checked Texaco's earnings for last year. They made just over fourteen billion dollars, so you can see how big a deal this is for them."

Air Products Corporation was a lesser-known giant of a company, with the lion's share of the market in purging chemicals and petrochemicals from the huge tanks industry uses for storing them, nationwide. I had no idea just how Air Products used natural gas, but I did know their Washington representative, Lewis Dale. The other two companies were major users of natural gas in Louisiana, as a key energy source and/or as a feedstock.

"Well," I began, "I know the Washington reps for all three of those companies. Give me a day or so to contact each of them and see if we can bring them on board with us."

"Make it one day if you can, Ed, and get back to me as soon as you know. Now, what're your plans for us to fight the Texaco language?"

I had thought about that ever since the previous call to Steder. "One thing I didn't mention yesterday was that one of the people at that NAM meeting was John Camp, Texaco's primary outside lawyer. My guess is that he had a hand in writing the direct sale language in the bill. He was sitting next to Don Annett, Texaco's Washington vice president."

"You mean outside lawyers can *do* that?" Steder asked.

"Hell yes. It happens all the time. They work with the staff of the members and the committees on the Hill, and with people in the president's administration as well. Anyway, Camp's firm is big in Louisiana. So I figure we should fight fire with fire, only with an even bigger fire. I'd like to see if we can get Patton, Boggs and Blow, Tommy Boggs's law firm, to represent us."

There was a pause while Steder digested this suggestion. Then, "Aren't they really expensive?"

"Oh yeah," I answered. "Tommy Boggs is a major rainmaker in this town. But if we want the best ..." (Tommy Boggs was the son of the late House majority leader Thomas Hale Boggs, Sr., Democrat from Louisiana, and of Lindy Boggs, who replaced her husband in Congress after he was lost in a small plane crash in Alaska eleven years earlier. Patton Boggs -- as it is familiarly known -- was perhaps the most prominent lobbying law firm in the city.)

"I know, I know," Steder interjected. "But be sure to make it clear to the other three companies that if they join us, this'll be a shared expense."

Steder's point was not unexpected. "Will do," I answered.

* * *

I didn't know Tommy Boggs personally. But as it happened, Phil Pulizzi, one of the other Washington reps in our office, knew someone else at Patton Boggs, a lawyer named Tim Vanderver. Phil called his contact and asked if we could set up a meeting with Boggs. I stood beside Phil as he made the call.

After a few moments, Phil covered the mouthpiece and said to me, "He wants to know how big an issue this is."

"Tell him it's an energy issue, and we're pretty sure it's major even by their standards." Pulizzi did so, listened and then turned to me and said, "He says they're likely to be willing to meet and see what we have in mind. Then they'll decide whether to work with us."

"Fair enough," I said. "Let's see if we can make it late tomorrow afternoon, after five." I figured it would take at least that long to bring the other companies on board with us.

Pulizzi spoke again to his contact, then hung up the phone and said, "You're on. He'll get back to me with the time. Do you need me there?"

"Will Vanderver be at the meeting?"

"Probably not. He'll likely clue in the partners and then stay out of it."

"Then, unless you feel you can add something different to the meeting, I'd really prefer we limit it to the Washington reps directly involved from each company."

"No problem. Happy to help."

"And Phil, many thanks, man."

CHAPTER FOUR

"THE MORE THE MERRIER"

MARCH 8 -- THE NEXT round of phone calls -- immediately after lunch -- were to Bob Cole, head of the Kaiser Aluminum and Chemical Washington office, Lewis Dale of Air Products and John Ferguson, from Georgia Pacific's Washington office. I rang up Cole and explained the situation, suggesting that he check with his energy and/or supply departments and then let me know what they had to say.

Bob Cole was a clear thinker with a speech pattern that tended to end every sentence on an upswing, as if he were asking a question. But his first comment actually was a question: "Are you *sure* about all this?"

"The only thing I know for sure is the impact on PPG, based on the enormous amount of natural gas we use every day at Lake Charles. But our energy supply man seems to think you guys are right up there with us in usage."

"That's a good enough starting point for me. You gonna be in later this afternoon, if I get a quick answer?"

"You bet."

Next on the call list was Lew Dale of Air Products, and the discussion went pretty much the same way as the previous one. Dale, a tall, sandy-haired, slender dry-witted guy, said he'd get back to me ASAP.

John Ferguson of Georgia Pacific was less enthusiastic. A taciturn man by nature, his first response was, "I really doubt that this deal is gonna affect us much at all, Ed."

"Well, why not just check with your folks and see what they have to say, John? Then let me know, okay?"

"I'll call them, but I'd be surprised if we join in any coalition."

"Fair enough," I concluded.

* * *

By four o'clock -- somewhat sooner than anticipated -- I had answers from Kaiser and Air Products.

An excited Bob Cole said, "Jesus, Ed, this bill could cost us over three hundred million dollars!"

I chuckled and replied, "Welcome to the club, Bob. That's just about the impact we reckon it would have on us."

Cole continued, "And if you haven't yet thought about how to approach the issue, I have some ideas." That didn't surprise me.

"Matter of fact," I replied, "we do have a tentative plan, but it would have to include your full involvement as well as that of any other companies affected by Texaco's proposal. It seems pretty clear that John Camp was intimately involved with writing Section 316 of the bill, the part that would clobber us."

Cole rejoined, "You know, of course, that Camp is also the personal attorney for Russell Long, right?"

"Yes, we did know about the relationship between Camp and Senator Long. And given that Long is the ranking member on the Senate

Finance Committee, to say nothing of his being Huey Long's son, he's a formidable force." (*The term "ranking member" is used to denote the top-ranking minority party member on any committee.*) I continued, "That's why I'd like to meet Camp head-on by hiring Tommy Boggs as our point man."

"I like it," Cole replied.

I explained, "In fact, we've already spoken with someone in Patton, Boggs about setting up a meeting in their offices for late tomorrow afternoon, after five. Could you make that meeting?"

"I'll be there. Just let me know the time."

"Oh, and by the way," I continued, "I have calls in to Air Products and Georgia Pacific as well, since our guy says they're likely in the same boat as you and we are."

"The more the merrier," said Cole. "In fact, since the bill's almost sure to be referred to the Senate Energy Committee, we ought to be thinking about which members of the committee each of our companies can contact. We might have reason to use that information at tomorrow's meeting."

"Agreed. We'll need to hit the ground at full speed if we're gonna stop this express."

Lew Dale called about half an hour later, and while he didn't offer the exact financial impact on Air Products, he said the more important words: "We're in." I briefed him about the calls to the other companies, including Bob Cole's idea, and about the planned meeting at Patton Boggs, and he agreed to join us there.

* * *

It was 11 a.m. the next morning and I was about to give up on Georgia Pacific when John Ferguson called.

"It'd be a big hit on us, something on the order of a hundred and twenty-five million. So what are we doing about it?"

I read him in on what we had done so far, including the Patton Boggs meeting. And now all the players were on board, and I was reaching for the phone to brief Bob Steder when Phil Pulizzi popped into the office and said the meeting at Patton, Boggs was on for 5:30. I asked Tena Stewart, our administrative assistant, to call back to the others while I phoned Steder with the news.

"Be sure to get some indication of how much the Boggs firm is gonna cost us, Ed. I've briefed Bill Harris, and he's on board with the idea, but he wants to know what the tab will be." Harris was the corporate vice president in charge of PPG's Chemical Division. (The company also had three other operating divisions at the time: Flat Glass, Fiber Glass and Coatings and Resins, including Pittsburgh Paints.)

I paused for a moment, then said, "Are you getting pressure from Chemical?" The Lake Charles plant was the crown jewel of the Chemical Division.

"Not yet. But we have to be within reason on all of our bills."

"Of course," I said, and thought little more of it.

CHAPTER FIVE

"IT'S YOUR GAME"

MARCH 8 -- AT 5:25 P. M., I walked through the front door of Patton, Boggs and Blow's posh suite at 25th and Pennsylvania Avenue, NW. The other three Washington reps in our group arrived shortly after.

We were escorted by a secretary into a conference room nearly as long as the cavernous meeting room at the National Association of Manufacturers, and met there by Tommy Boggs and another member of the firm. Probably every Washington representative in the city would recognize Tommy Boggs on sight: about six feet, with curly dark hair and carrying a few extra pounds.

Boggs immediately strode over to us. Extending his hand to me, he said, "Hi, Ed Jaffee. You went to Wilson High and Bullis Prep a few years before I was at Georgetown Prep."

Talk about being speechless! I still don't know which junior staffer had mined this information for the boss, or why he focused on our DC-area high schools, but if the object was to catch me off guard, it succeeded handsomely. "I, uh, I guess so, if that's what you say," I blurted inanely, immediately feeling massively inadequate. "I had heard you went to Georgetown Prep."

But by that time, Tommy was already working the other three guys in our group. He knew a relevant point or two about each one, and their smiles at my discomfort immediately faded. It was clear that we were on his turf, and not just geographically.

Then, reversing course to put us all at ease, Boggs continued, "Let's have a drink. What are your choices?" he asked, heading toward a credenza at the far end of the room. He pushed a button and the credenza morphed into a well-stocked bar. As he turned back toward us, Boggs noticed my quizzical look and added, "It's after office hours, Ed." I silently kicked myself for showing surprise.

As we took our seats at the table, Boggs introduced us to the other attorney in the room. "This is Bill Foster, one of our best men, a partner, and an expert on energy issues. Assuming we agree to work with you folks, I've asked Bill to be your main point of contact."

Then, reading our collective minds, he added, "But I'll be involved as well, as necessary. Now, tell us about your problem."

It took ten minutes for the four of us to brief Boggs and Foster, during which time the two men listened impassively. I was beginning to wonder if Patton Boggs would come on board with us, when Foster spoke up: "We'll need a champion, someone with the clout to be a lead player on this, and also with ties to the state."

A broad smile came over Tommy Boggs's face. "Now, you wouldn't be thinking about Bennett, would you, Bill?"

Foster was a tall, trim middle-aged man with a hint of a soft Southern accent and wavy graying hair. Keeping a straight face, he responded, "Yes indeed. Bennett Johnston, the junior senator from Louisiana, and also the ranking Democrat on the Senate Energy Committee."

In the spirit of the dialogue, I chimed in, "And you guys might just happen to know the good senator, right?"

Boggs replied dryly, "You could say that. So, Bill, I'll get involved here at the start and then you'll carry the ball, okay?"

Foster nodded, and Boggs left, as we pondered what his specific involvement would be. Foster made small talk. After ten minutes, it was beginning to look like another psychological ploy on their part, when Tommy Boggs strode back into the room and said, "It's set. You'll meet with Bennett Johnston at 4 p.m. tomorrow." He shook all our hands and added, "It's your game, Bill."

As we were leaving, I turned to Foster, "I assume Tommy spoke directly with the senator?"

"No. I'd bet he set it up through his mother. Given the stakes in Louisiana, it's better for the request to come from another member of the state congressional delegation."

CHAPTER SIX

"OUR COMMITTEE WORKS COLLEGIALLY"

MARCH 9 -- THERE WERE a couple of housekeeping duties for me to tend to before we would meet with Senator Johnston. First, I called Bob Steder and told him we would need to brief our Law Department on the situation. Bob quickly set up a three-way call and reached Dick Packard, PPG's general counsel.

Packard listened silently, then asked the question I figured he would: "Do we really need outside counsel on this one?"

"It's a potentially disastrous situation for us," Steder replied. And I added, "Dick, it gives us the best chance to win. You know how big Boggs is in this town."

There was a pause, followed by "Alright. But watch their billing like a hawk."

Immediately after that call, I phoned Bill Foster. "Bill," I began, "we'll obviously need to know what your billing fees are, per hour."

"Of course," came the reply. "I'll send over a letter making it official, but for now, here's how we work it. Tommy bills at $250 per hour, and I and the other senior partners bill at $225. We'll want to include Bill O'Hara. He's of counsel to the firm *(employed by the firm, but not as a partner or an associate; a not-unusual situation with former Members of Congress)* and a former House member from Michigan, and he'll be an asset on the House version of this legislation. His rate is $200, and there'll be some associate attorneys and paralegals involved from time to time."

"What're their fees?"

"The junior members of the firm have varying fees, but on average, it's about $125 to $150, with the paralegals doing research. Their rate is $60 an hour. Oh, and we bill in six-minute increments." (Translated to 2010 rates for major lobbying law firms, these fees would be well over twice as high. Even so, in 1983 Tommy Boggs's fee would've covered more than half of my monthly mortgage.)

I closed my eyes and saw dollar signs winging off into the distance, but said only, "Well, let's see the rate sheet and we'll take it from there. And Bill, I plan to ask the other three companies to be equal partners in this thing."

"I figured you would," said Foster. "I'll get the letter over to you today. We'll plan to use you as the initial billing point, and let you parcel it out however you choose, okay?"

"Seems logical," I answered, and then immediately wondered about the best way to frame the request to Bob Cole of Kaiser, Lew Dale of Air Products and Georgia Pacific's John Ferguson.

After those phone calls, I drafted an internal memo for the key people in PPG management, briefing them on the situation and on what we had done so far. I knew Steder would have already filled in his boss, John Brownell, VP of Supply for the company, but included Brownell, as well as Bill Harris, the head man in the Chemical Division. The cc list included Stan Williams, PPG's board chairman and CEO; Dick Packard; Frank O'Neil, the VP of Government and Public Affairs; Steder and my immediate boss, Gary Wilson, head of the Washington office, whom I had kept in the loop from the start.

I had never before copied-in Williams or Harris on an action plan memo, but then, this was no ordinary issue.

*　*　*

Cole, Dale, Ferguson, Bill Foster and I sat in the reception area of Senator Johnston's office on the first floor of the Philip Hart Senate Office Building. After several minutes, Energy Committee staff counsel Daryl Owen and Betsy Moeller, Johnston's key legislative assistant for energy issues (and later head of the Federal Energy Regulatory Commission), came out and ushered us into the senator's office.

All of the Washington reps in our group had met Senator Johnston previously, not surprising given our stake in Louisiana. What did surprise us was the fifth man who walked in just as we were taking our seats. He was George White, and it turned out he was a vice president of the largest utility company in the state, Louisiana Power & Light, or LP&L.

"Aftuhnoon, Senatuh," he said, walking past us with his hand outstretched. "Good to see you."

Johnston rose from his seat, reached across the desk and gave this latest visitor a warm handshake before settling back. To Johnston, Bill Foster said, "I believe you've met the other fellows here," naming us. Then he added, "Tommy and I thought it might be a good idea to ask George to sit in on this meeting."

I was surprised that our outside attorney hadn't briefed us beforehand, but as soon as White told us his title, it was apparent he might be a major help, depending on LP&L's natural gas supply source.

George White was a slight, slender man, perhaps five-seven or at best five-eight, with reddish blond hair. But the most arresting thing about him was his seeming youth. With what still looked like peach-fuzz on his cheeks, he might have passed for a Capitol page instead of a vice president of a major utility. As we learned shortly, looks can be deceiving.

Foster led the discussion as he explained our concerns with the proposed language in the Senate bill. Without being exact, he emphasized that the economic impact on our four companies would be "in the many hundreds of millions of dollars, and thousands of Louisiana jobs could be at stake."

Johnston listened impassively, then replied, "Well, I dunno, fellas. I had dinner late last night with John McKinley, Texaco's board chairman, and he seems to think you guys have had pretty much of a free ride the last ten years or so. He thinks it's only fair that since other companies in the state are paying the full market rate for natural gas, you guys should be paying your fair share as well."

Several emotions were racing through my mind. First, how in hell did Texaco find out so soon that we were working with Tommy Boggs and seeing Johnston? Then, almost at the same moment, it struck me that Johnston's staff must have called Texaco as soon as they had agreed to meet with us. The senator needed to know both sides of the issue as early as possible. And Texaco was playing hardball if their chairman immediately took the company jet to Washington to meet with Johnston. So, was the senator going to bail on us, despite the link to Tommy and Lindy Boggs?

Before Bill Foster or any of our group could respond, little George White spoke up, in a decided Southern accent: "Wayull, Bennett, Ah guess we could live with the huge increase in cost. Of co-ess, we'd have to pass it own to the residential ratepayuhs." That meant the majority of residents in the state.

That's how we learned that LP&L also had a long-term, low-cost contract with Texaco. What we didn't yet know was that their contract ran through 1992, and that the bite on their company would approximate a staggering two billion dollars.

But Senator Johnston knew. He knew full well. And he was up for re-election the following year. He reddened slightly, and then, a bit flustered, responded, "Well now, George, don't, don't, I don't want you folks gettin' too upset over this." Then, more calmly, he said to all of us, "Look, tell you what. This is just one small part of a huge piece of legislation. I realize it's major to all of your companies, but it's one section in a bill of more than three hundred sections. So here's what I propose to do. Our committee works collegially. Jim McClure, Wendell Ford and I have been planning to get together to go over the entire bill next week, and I'll include your concerns in that discussion." (*James McClure, chairman of the Senate Energy Committee, was an Idaho Republican, while Ford, a Kentucky Democrat, was a longtime power on the panel.*)

"Can we assume you'll see our side of the issue, senator, including the matter of sanctity of contract?" It was Foster who asked the key question.

"I think that's a fair assumption," Johnston responded.

* * *

As we filed into the outer office, I turned to George White and said, "Welcome to our ad hoc coalition." Clearly, White had pulled our chestnuts out of the fire.

"Thanks, but LP&L would rathuh work alone own this one. If it's okay with you guys, let's keep each othuh in the loop as things move along. Okay?"

Foster answered for us: "Of course, George." I was thinking that Patton, Boggs had already earned their fee by arranging the Johnston meeting and bringing White into the session.

The rest of the group decided to go back to my office at PPG. Along the way, Bob Cole turned to Foster and, agreeing with my earlier thought, said, "Thanks for asking White to the meeting."

"Well, Bennett needed to know what LP&L's reaction would be."

"I'm just glad he found out," I concluded.

CHAPTER SEVEN

A HELL OF A LOT OF TERRITORY

MARCH 9 -- BACK AT the PPG offices on Rhode Island Avenue, NW, just off of Connecticut Avenue, it was time for us to begin scoping out the plan of attack for our lobbying efforts. Given the significance of this issue to PPG, I had been freed up to focus fulltime on it. I asked the other three Washington reps if they were also working solely on this issue. Dale and Turner said yes, while Cole said he had a few other, smaller issues, but that this one took precedence over everything else.

There were twenty-two members of the Senate Energy Committee and forty-two on the House Energy and Commerce Committee, the two groups with original jurisdiction over the Reagan administration's natural gas decontrol bill. Add to that the leadership of the House and Senate, including the House Rules Committee, and we knew we had some heavy lifting to do.

(The House Rules Committee has responsibility for deciding the rules under which a bill will be considered on the House floor; will it be open to amendments at all points -- a so-called "open rule" -- or open to amendments only at specified points -- a "modified open rule" -- or will it be closed to all amendments, calling for a straight yea or nay vote on the House floor?)

None of us could predict how soon the legislation would have subcommittee consideration, much less reaching the full committee in each house of Congress, but regardless of the timing, Bob Cole reasoned, "Let's assume Senator Johnston gets McClure and Ford to agree to delete or at least change Texaco's language. That'll mean a full-court press by Texaco to have the language reinserted either before or during markup in the Energy Committee. *("Markup" is the term used to describe the process of amending a bill, usually taking it section-by-section, in committee.)* So we do need to be ready to hit the Hill, together with Bill. Meanwhile, let's wait a few days to see how Texaco's language is changed or deleted."

Foster added, "Absolutely. We wait until Bennett meets with McClure and Ford."

Ferguson countered, "Yes, but let's figure out our four companies' assignments now, so we're ready to start moving when we do get the word."

With that, we looked at the 22-member Senate Energy Committee and found ten of them in whose states our group had manufacturing facilities. As it happened, PPG was in six of those states: Louisiana, already covered by Patton Boggs and the other members of our group; Pennsylvania (PPG is headquartered in Pittsburgh, while Air Products is based in Allentown), represented by Sen. John Heinz; Ohio, represented by Sen. Howard Metzenbaum; Oklahoma, represented by Sen. Don Nickles and where PPG had a modest-sized flat glass manufacturing plant; Texas, with Sen. Lloyd Bentsen; and Georgia, whose member on the committee was Sen. Sam Nunn. I said I would take those six states, but John Ferguson pointed out Georgia Pacific's obvious strong ties to that state. We agreed that John would see Senator Nunn first, with a follow-up visit including me if necessary.

But our coalition had contacts -- though not facilities -- in several others states on the committee, so the list of assignments looked like this (with the lead coalition member listed first):

Sen. Lloyd Bentsen (D-TX) - Ed Jaffee, Patton Boggs;

Sen. Dale Bumpers (D-AR) – John Ferguson – Georgia-Pacific had facilities in Arkansas;

Sen. Thad Cochran (R-MS) – We thought George White might have a contact in the office;

Sen. Wendell Ford (D-KY) – Bill Foster would touch base, mainly to thank the senator for his role in protecting us in the redrafting of the bill;

Sen. Henry ("Scoop") Jackson (D-WA) – John Ferguson;

Sen. Bennett Johnston (D-LA) – Patton Boggs and all of us;

Sen. Sam Nunn (D-GA) – John Ferguson, then Ed Jaffee or possibly a group visit;

Sen. Bill Bradley (D-NJ) – Patton Boggs; also, Ed Jaffee (This was a long shot for me, in that a Missouri bank that Bradley's father had owned had provided the initial loan to start up PPG's large glass plant in the state years earlier);

Sen. Mark Hatfield (R-OR) – John Ferguson - Georgia-Pacific was big in the state;

Sen. John Heinz (R-PA) – Lew Dale, Ed Jaffee;

Sen. Howard Metzenbaum (D-OH) – Ed Jaffee;

Sen. Frank Murkowski, (R-AK) – Patton Boggs;

Chairman James McClure (R-ID) – Patton Boggs, in consultation with Bennett Johnston;

Sen. Don Nickles (R-OK) – Ed Jaffee;

Sen. Ted Stevens (R-AK) – Patton Boggs;

Sen. John Warner (R-VA) – Bob Cole knew the senator fairly well.

Senators with whom we had no ties were Pete Domenici (R-NM), Carl

Levin (D-MI), Spark Matsunaga (D-HI), John Melcher (R-MT), Malcolm Wallop (R-WY) and Lowell Weicker (R-CT).

With fifteen -- or possibly sixteen if we included Cochran -- of the twenty-two members of the Energy Committee included, I turned to Bob Cole, "Kaiser doesn't have facilities in any of these states, though as you said, you do know Senator Warner, right?"

"Warner, yes, but as for the others, other than Louisiana, no," Cole replied. "But I know Daryl Owen, Senator Johnston's man on the Energy Committee staff, pretty well, and there are members of the House Energy and Commerce Committee whose districts include a few of our facilities. So I can start working that side of the Hill as soon as we want."

"Well," I said, "sounds like we have the Senate Energy Committee reasonably well covered."

"Hold on," cautioned Foster. "Never, ever assume anything in this business. First place, we may need multiple visits to these people and their staffs. Second, we'll want to stay close to the Energy Committee staff." Then, warming to his subject, he added, "Third, we'll probably need to talk with the Department of Energy. Fourth," he continued, nodding to Cole, "we need to get moving on analyzing the House version of the legislation. Is it a companion bill, or are there substantive differences? We need to know that before Bob here and the rest of us can start those meetings." *(A "companion" bill is one that exactly mirrors the version introduced in the other body of Congress.)* "And fifth," Foster concluded, "when the time comes, we'll need to think about talking with the members of the House Rules Committee."

"We realize that," Lew Dale responded, speaking for the group. "But don't you think we should focus our efforts first on the Senate Energy Committee?"

"I'm not saying we don't do that," replied Foster. "It's just that there's a hell of a lot of territory to cover, and we should be using these next few days to plan how we're gonna do that."

All four of us nodded, and then Bill Foster added a surprise: "One of our smaller clients is CF Industries, an agricultural chemicals co-operative represented here by Rosemary O'Brien. Word travels fast in Washington, and Rosemary called me this morning. She said she had heard about our ad hoc coalition, and mentioned that she and Russell King, who represents Freeport-McMoRan, a good-sized minerals exploration and production company that's big in Louisiana, had just formed a group of their own to work on the same bill."

"I know about Freeport," I offered. "They used to be called Freeport Sulfur, and then Freeport Minerals. So what about them and the others? Are they in our camp?"

"Well, most of the folks in their group are agricultural chemicals manufacturers, and while their contracts with Texaco and other natural gas suppliers are smaller than ours, they would all be hurt if Texaco's language stayed in the bill. That language would apply to intrastate contracts in quite a few states, not just in Louisiana."

"You say 'they would *all* be hurt,'" Bob Cole interjected. "Who else is in their group?"

"From what I know so far, it includes First Mississippi and Mississippi Chemical, CF Industries, Freeport McMoRan and, to a smaller degree, Borden Chemical. Oh, and they knew about LP&L, and Rosemary had phoned George White. He told her the same thing he told us, about being a free agent, but said he'd like to be included in any meetings between our two coalitions. And by the way, First Mississippi and Mississippi Chemical are both agri-chemicals firms."

Foster may or may not have noticed the surprised look on my face. Was *anything* being kept close to the vest in this deal? At any rate, Bill's next comment was, "Look. We're all after the same end result here. We've seen what George White can do. Some of you guys may know one or more of the local players for these companies. And I know they often work with different law firms. But the point remains, their resources can expand our efforts. I told Rosemary O'Brien that this morning, and said I'd brief our coalition on her group's willingness to work with us." In fact, Ferguson and I were friendly with Freeport McMoRan's Russell King, who had formerly been staff director to Sen. Howell Heflin of Alabama.

"Makes sense," answered Cole, as the rest of us nodded.

With that, Bill Foster said, "It's time I headed back to the firm. I'll call you guys as soon as we have word from Senator Johnston."

I knew it was time to broach the matter of paying for the Boggs firm, and asked the other three Washington reps to hang back as Foster was leaving. Bill paused, gave me what I took as a knowing smile, then left.

Lew Dale said, "Well, Ed, since you formed the coalition, I take it there's a reason for this."

"Oh yeah," I replied. "Actually, two reasons, and both involve housekeeping matters. First, while I did form the coalition, I think the best approach would be for me to be the facilitator, in an unofficial manner, rather than being chair of the group. And in the same vein, I suggest we rotate the meeting locations to each of our offices."

"To be a moving target?" Dale said, half to himself.

"Well, more to keep Texaco and John Camp off-guard as to who's running this show," I answered. My hidden agenda was to get the other three companies to feel co-ownership of the coalition, in hopes that doing so would make it more likely they would be willing to share the costs.

Cole was right on top of things, as he nodded. "And I think I know the other thing you wanted to discuss. It's who's paying for the Boggs firm, right?"

My broad smile may have been a bit too obvious as I immediately agreed. I filled the other three in on my discussion with Bob Steder, adding, "It's obvious Tommy Boggs and his team won't come cheap. I did take the liberty of getting a rate list faxed over from Foster this morning." I walked over to my desk and pulled out three copies.

The other three surveyed the rates with impassive faces, so I continued, "Obviously, you'll want to run this past your own companies. FYI, I contacted our Law Department this morning as well as Bob Steder. And Steder had already brought our Chemical Group into the picture."

"And what did they say?" It was Lew Dale who asked.

Figuring candor was the right approach, I chuckled. "They all said this is a major issue for us. And then they told me to get the other three players to split the fee." Their smiles were barely perceptible, but all three agreed to check with their companies and get back to me, hopefully within the next day or so. With that, we adjourned, relieved to have another group of companies in the arena with us against Texaco.

As it turned out, we would need them in the months to come.

CHAPTER EIGHT

A VALUABLE ASSET

MARCH 11 -- WHILE OUR coalition was waiting to hear from Senator Johnston, Texaco had not been sitting still. Johnston, feeling he owed it to Texaco, had informed their chairman, John McKinley, of the impending meeting among himself and Senators McClure and Ford. I was alerted by a phone call from Sara Schotland, an attorney with PPG's outside counsel on retainer, Cleary, Gottlieb, Steen and Hamilton, that an unnamed source had told them Texaco was preparing a letter to all senators on the Senate Energy Committee, presumably to be delivered by Don Annett.

By this time, I was long inured to surprise at the wildfire speed with which word spread in Washington. I asked Sara how she found out about our coalition and was told that our general counsel, Dick Packard, had briefed her. Doing so was, of course, his perfect right. Still, I phoned Packard later and gently reminded him that we were all on the same team and should make sure all the players stayed in the loop. He agreed, and in fact, this was virtually the only time I felt in any way blindsided by anything anyone else in PPG had done.

Then I phoned Steder and told him I was calling a meeting of the "First Four" -- as we informally began calling ourselves after the five other companies plus LP&L became involved -- and asked if we shouldn't include Sara Schotland in that meeting. Bob quickly agreed, and Tena Stewart placed the calls.

* * *

Schotland proved valuable right from the start. She had begun researching our case the night before, and showed up at PPG for our meeting carrying a memo to me, Bob Steder and Dick Packard. The piece covered Texaco's statements at a December,1977, State of Louisiana hearing. At the hearing, Texaco had made these points, among others:

They recognized that companies built industrial plants in reliance on Texaco's long-term natural gas supply obligation and that those companies employ a large number of people;

They said the contracts were favorable to Texaco when entered into, basically affirming what Steder had told me about their annual report from 1967;

They acknowledged, with prescience, that they had anticipated a shortfall in delivery of natural gas by "at least" 1973; and, most importantly to us,

Texaco said it recognized it had an obligation and must "meet the commitments" of its customers. It was a tiny step between that phrase and Foster's argument of sanctity of contract.

After quickly reading the memo, I thanked Sara and told her I was making copies to share with Cole, Dale and Ferguson. Cole flipped through the two pages and commented, "And this was written well after Texaco's failed effort in 1973-74 to abrogate our contracts."

"That's true," I added, "and it gives us a good piece of ammunition to use in our lobbying." Then, turning to Schotland, I asked, "Is it okay if Bill Foster of the Boggs firm sees this? He'll be doing a fair portion of our visits on the Hill, and at some point, he'll probably see Senator Long."

"It's your call, Ed. We're on retainer to PPG." Then she added, "You might want to run it past Dick Packard first."

"Right," I said. Cleary Gottlieb was retained by Packard and our Law Department.

"Speaking of Foster," asked Ferguson, "any idea when they expect word back from Johnston and the others about the reworked bill?"

"Not that I've heard," I responded.

From the quizzical look on Schotland's face it was apparent that Packard had not brought her up to date on our visit with Senator Johnston, so I took the opportunity to do so, including George White of Louisiana Power & Light's part in the meeting. Sara's immediate reaction was to think ahead. "It seems to me that Johnston, McClure and Ford could take any one of several avenues to resolve our issue. They could simply delete Texaco's language, of course. But there may be other players in this game, companies or residential consumers that would be hurt by part, but not all, of the language."

"How do you mean," asked Cole.

"Well, for example, take the terms 'first sale,' 'direct sale' and 'not for resale.' All of those terms apply to PPG and, I assume, to the rest of you?" The other three nodded.

"Okay," Schotland continued, "but what if there are companies that don't meet all three of those conditions, but just one or two of them? The members of the Senate Energy Committee may have relationships with one or more of those folks as well as with you four."

"So," Cole asked, "how would that work?"

"Well," came the answer, "take the intrastate local distribution companies. They're the ones, like Washington Gas Light in our area for example, who buy natural gas from intrastate producers via the gas pipelines and then provide it to the end users, reselling it in the process. They'd certainly want to be sure their own contracts would not in any way be jeopardized by whatever language ends up in this bill."

"Whoa!" It was Cole who interjected. "From what you say, I don't see that those people would be hurt. But the wrong kind of language could conceivably cost us LP&L, and we sure as hell can't afford to lose *them*!"

"Exactly," said Schotland. "So my point is that we have to be prepared for several different wordings when the senators are done with their review."

"Well, that's what we have you for," I said to Sara. "And I'm assuming the rest of you will want to check with your own corporate and outside lawyers as well."

Cole nodded. Dale smiled. Ferguson arched a brow.

With that, we decided to adjourn until we received word from Bill Foster.

CHAPTER NINE

"A CAP ON OUR COMMITMENT"

MARCH 17 --THE PHONE call from Foster came at 10:25 a.m.

"Okay, Ed, I just got the word from Daryl Owen. Johnston, Chairman McClure and Ford spent yesterday afternoon and evening fine-tooth-combing much of the bill, and there's good news for us."

My initial reaction was palpable relief. But then, remembering Sara Schotland's caution, I said, "What's the exact wording?"

"How about if I come over to your office and go over it with you and the other guys?"

"Okay," I said, "but let's see if we can hold this one at Bob Cole's office. We've agreed to share hosting of the meetings. And I'll ask Sara Schotland to attend as well. You saw the Texaco paper she found for us."

There was a slight pause, and then Foster said, "That's fine with me. So can I assume you're still chairing the group?"

"I suggested we use 'facilitator' instead. And we've agreed to rotate the meeting places, as a way to keep the Camp firm just a bit off guard." I didn't add the part about hoping to encourage the others to share the Boggs firm's fees.

Foster laughed. "I suspect it'll take a good bit more than that to keep John Camp off guard. But it's your show. So how about you pick a time and call me with the address?"

As I put down the phone, I realized I'd heard nothing yet from the others about fee-sharing. I called Bob Cole, gave him the news that the language had been reworked, and asked if our group could meet at his offices at Connecticut Avenue and I Street. He agreed and we set a 3 p.m. meeting, with Cole's office to call the other three men, while I would call Sara Schotland.

I added, "It'd be really helpful to know, Bob, if Kaiser has agreed to split the fees with us and the others, for the Boggs firm."

"Oh, yeah, sorry I hadn't gotten back to you on that. We'll chip in, but our Law Department put a thirty thousand dollar cap on our commitment."

"Jeez, Bob, thirty thousand likely won't go far at all, given the level of response we expect Texaco to mount once they see this new language."

"I know, Ed, and I'm pretty sure that if the issue goes farther than our lawyers hope it will, I can convince them to keep us in the game."

"Okay," I responded. "I'll call Foster and invite him to the meeting." Fee-sharing or not, I needed to continue as the key contact point with Patton Boggs.

After calling Foster, I picked up the phone again, this time to brief Steder on Kaiser's decision on cost-sharing. Neither of us felt reassured about who would pay what portion of the legal fees, but I told Steder I would press Lew Dale and John Ferguson and get back to him when I had definitive numbers.

That left only the call to Dick Packard to let him know I needed to share the memo Schotland had prepared for us, with Foster. Packard asked if that was okay with Sara, and I told him she was on board with it if he had no objections. We decided to do so -- a good thing for me, since I had forgotten to call Packard before arranging to have Bill at the afternoon meeting.

* * *

MARCH 18, 3 P.M. -- Bob Cole convened the meeting and we immediately got down to business, as Foster distributed copies of the proposed amending language to each of us. As we began reading, Bill provided background: "Bennett and the others had several constituencies to consider in coming up with this language. They ultimately decided on a narrowly crafted fix, to limit the 'market out' provisions to intrastate natural gas that is sold for resale."

Sara Schotland smiled slightly but said nothing.

"Wait a minute." I said, "Let me be sure I have this right. Wouldn't that screw the local distribution companies, who take the gas they buy and resell it to the consumer? And if so, wouldn't LP&L be adamantly opposed to that language?"

"Hold on. Slow down, Ed," countered Foster. Read the next line and you'll see there's an exemption for intrastate local distribution companies."

And indeed there was. So it appeared that the "for resale" language would affect intrastate resales involving industrial customers only.

Lew Dale beat me to the punch on the next point: "Won't this look like a transparent fix for LP&L?" I was about to say, "It looks as if George White's been scoring points again."

"Not when you consider the dozens of local distributors in states that receive intrastate natural gas," answered Foster. "This amendment, as crafted, should assure the support -- or at least non-opposition -- of all the members in the Senate and House whose states have intrastate natural gas and who want to help the consumer as the end-user. That's a fair number of states."

The four of us spent the next half hour playing devil's advocate, looking for holes in the amending language. Foster effectively countered every point we raised.

"Won't this look like a major gift to our companies and others like us, as opposed to the rest of Texaco's customers? I mean, isn't this opening us up to the argument Texaco's chairman made to Senator Johnston, that our companies have been getting a free ride on today's natural gas prices, compared with other companies in Louisiana?" It was Ferguson who raised this point.

"Look," replied Foster, "the first counter to that argument is the need to retain sanctity of contracts. And second, you guys have all been around long enough to know that in virtually every compromise there are gonna be winners and losers. In this case, the public is protected and we come out winners."

"I guess," said Cole, "it really comes down to the fact that our group was hoping to find that section totally deleted from the bill."

"I realize that," replied Foster. "And when Daryl Owen called me late yesterday to say they were leaning toward this language, I did raise the same point. But he said that McClure, Johnston and Ford preferred this kind of a narrow fix instead. They felt it would be easier to defend in the committee markup."

Schotland added, "As these guys know, I had anticipated the possibility of something of this sort. And I agree with you, Bill, that it can work for us."

"Well," Cole conceded, "then I guess that's what we go with, and it's certainly far better than what was there before."

With that, Foster headed back to Patton Boggs, and Schotland also left the meeting.

* * *

It was time to ask Air Products and Georgia Pacific if they were ready to split the Boggs firm's legal fees. John Ferguson surprised me by immediately nodding agreement. "So that's a yes?" I asked.

"That's a yes."

I turned to Lew Dale, who said, "We're in", then added, "but let's try hard to keep the costs within reason, okay?" I told Dale we were both on the same page in that regard and that he sounded like our Law Department.

Later, in the PPG offices, I briefed Steder on the just-concluded meeting. After giving him the good news about Georgia Pacific and Air Products agreeing to the fee-split, I outlined the proposed amending language. He initially doubted the wording's usefulness but grudgingly agreed after I told him we first shared his concern but realized the Johnston-McClure-Ford fix was the best we could get.

"So will this make your lobbying job more difficult?"

"If Foster is right, it might make things a bit easier for us because it protects the public consumers of intrastate gas, though I'm not really sure it'll be easier at this point. But look, it's still way too early to play the prediction game, Bob. This whole situation, like any major piece of legislation, may have several twists and turns before it's finished."

"Well," Steder said, "that's what we pay you guys the big bucks for."

I chuckled and replied, "If only that were true."

CHAPTER TEN

A FAR WIDER PLAYING FIELD

MARCH 21 --TEXACO HAD wasted no time in responding to the new language in the Senate bill. Clearly, Senator Johnston had told them about the changes. Bill Foster briefed me on that fact, adding that our opponent had delivered a letter to all members of the Senate Energy Committee, reiterating the points they had made to Senator Johnston. I made a note to add this information to the agenda for our next group meeting. We expected continued sharply increased pressure from Texaco.

Meanwhile, Sara Schotland and her team at Cleary, Gottleib were going full bore on the case, probably pressed by Dick Packard. Early the next morning, she dropped by and presented me with a one-page lawyerly analysis and point paper with a heading that read like the title of a PhD dissertation: "Contracts for the First Sale of Natural Gas to End-Users in the Intrastate Market Should Not Be Subject to Abrogation."

The Cleary Gottleib paper pointed out that during the period before passage of the Natural Gas Policy Act of 1977 – the law the current bill would amend – intrastate contracts with end-users were executed by producers and end-users in at least 24 states. That presented a far wider playing field than I had realized. But the point of the paper was that unlike the vast majority of producer-pipeline contracts, these end-user contracts were the result of arms-length negotiations between the parties and were not predicated on federal regulation. That fact, augmented by Texaco's own comments about honoring their commitments, at that 1977 State of Louisiana hearing, might score some solid points for us. I quickly got copies over to the other Washington representatives.

* * *

MARCH 22 -- With Congress's Easter recess coming up, from Friday, April 1, through Sunday, April 10, we were moving into high gear. The "First Four" and Bill Foster each had our assignments; it was time to hit Capitol Hill, and specifically the Senate Energy Committee, formally called the Energy and Natural Resources Committee. After a quick breakfast at Lew Dale's office, the corporate reps grabbed a cab and set off. Foster drove on his own, and we agreed to meet for a 12:30 lunch in as quiet a corner as we could find in the Philip Hart Senate Office Building cafeteria.

My initial visits were to the energy issue legislative aides to Senators Bentsen of Texas and Nickles of Oklahoma. Foster could join me on a follow-up trip to see Bentsen, or possibly Tommy Boggs could make that contact. The calls on all the senators themselves could come later, allowing the aides time to brief their principals and the senators time to review the entire reworked bill with their staff.

For most Washington representatives, it is generally a good idea to work first with a member of Congress's staff before seeing the member himself or herself. The exception, of course, would be those instances in which the Washington rep or outside attorney is personally close to the member, but even then, it's best to at least check in first with the key staffer. A good staffer will have the ear of his or her boss, and a seasoned Washington representative knows the importance of assisting the staffer with as much supporting information as possible.

Depending on the issue, it is sometimes also wise to be prepared to brief the case for the other side, as a way of showing that you fully understand the issue. And often the most important factor is having knowledge of the likely political implications of what you're asking the member to do in supporting your position.

It was not lost on me that my first visits were to be with two members unlikely to support us. After all, Texas and Oklahoma were major "oil patch" states, and Texaco had a strong presence in both of them.

So I was not surprised when Sen. Bentsen's legislative aide was noncommittal, saying only that she was sure there were two sides to the situation. I said I knew Texaco would take the other side, and the staffer then wondered aloud where Senator Long might come down on the issue. The question was not surprising, given Long's position as ranking member of the Senate Finance Committee and the fact that at some point, every senator had an interest in taxation issues, which come before that committee.

Knowing that Tommy Boggs was close to both Senators Bentsen and Long, I replied only that, "The Boggs firm will of course be in touch with the senator, as will all four of our companies." I left her with two one-page briefs, the Cleary Gottlieb paper Sara had just furnished, and one prepared by Bill Foster, focusing heavily on the sanctity of contract argument. The thrust of that argument was that allowing Texaco to unilaterally breach these contracts would set a dangerous precedent across the spectrum of all energy contracts, one that had the potential to throw the whole natural gas market into chaos.

We ended the session by agreeing that PPG and perhaps others would call to set up a meeting with the senator "within the next few weeks." We would save Texaco's 1977 position paper for that meeting.

From there, it was a five-minute walk to Sen. Nickles' office, where I met with the senator's legislative aide for energy issues. We had hardly begun the conversation when he said, "I understand your coalition plans to see just about every member of the committee."

This thing is becoming something of a cause célèbre, I thought, but said only, "I'm sure Texaco is planning the same thing."

"Matter of fact, they were in here the other day," the aide countered.

"And I've got a pretty good idea what they said."

"Let's leave what they said to them. What's your take on the matter?"

I talked him through our position papers and left, feeling certain we would not have Nickles' vote.

* * *

There was still an hour before our lunch meeting, so I found a phone at the National Democratic Club on the Hill (the company had memberships in both major party's clubs) and reported in to Steder.

"Not a good start," he began, and I agreed, but added that we knew Nickles and especially Bentsen would likely be hard sells. "And as you would expect, I'm sure Texaco's top management has already contacted both senators. Now, that doesn't mean they're a totally lost cause. There's still some time before the Energy Committee considers the bill."

Steder wondered, "How will that work?"

"Well, often but not necessarily, a committee will hold hearings on an issue before moving to mark up a bill. In this case, it's the Reagan administration that introduced the bill, using Chairman McClure as the key sponsor. It's a major public policy issue, so I'd anticipate there'll be hearings at both the subcommittee and full committee levels. I can't see many members missing a chance for the news coverage."

"And after the hearings?"

"At that point they hold the committee markup." Steder knew that markup was the time when amendments would be considered.

"Any idea when the process will start?"

"We have the Boggs firm trying to dope that out right now," I answered. "Soon as I know, you'll know."

CHAPTER ELEVEN

"SCORE-CARDING"

MARCH 22 -- THE REPORTS from Dale and Ferguson were somewhat more favorable than mine. Ferguson had been busy, setting up an appointment with Nunn's staff and seeing the legislative aides for Senators Bumpers of Arkansas and Jackson of Washington. John reported that George White had already been in to talk with the Bumpers staff; it turned out that LP&L's parent company, Middle South Utilities, was also a major player in Arkansas. Bumpers told Ferguson he was "favorably disposed" toward our position.

Scoop Jackson's staffer noted that the senator was ailing and staff wasn't sure when he would return, but said he would be sure to get our arguments to him as soon as possible.

I couldn't help indulging in the pointless game -- at this early stage -- of "score-carding," thinking to myself that this likely meant one in favor and probably two opposed to us, with one in the "undecided" column.

Patton Boggs' ties with Senator Murkowski were close enough that Bill Foster merely checked briefly with the senator's chief of staff before going into the office. "It's too soon to say how the senator will vote," Foster reported, "but he did say he agreed that major changes to the Natural Gas Policy Act were needed, and added that he was opposed to what he called major marketplace disruptions. I reminded him that the Texaco position would certainly lead to a major disruption."

So, list Murkowski as undecided.

Even though Senators Johnston and Heinz were the only members on Lew Dale's list to visit, Lew decided to stop by Sen. Weicker of Connecticut's office, reasoning that Air Products provided the nitrogen to purge hundreds of petroleum and chemical tanks in the state. Lew's company could say the same of most other states in the country, but Weicker was one of the committee members in whose state none of us had plants or labs.

Dale reported that Weicker's staff had been contacted by Texaco, but had offered no specifics on that visit. After Lew made the case for our position, the legislative aide allowed as how the senator was "a long way from making a decision on this issue." Lew left him the briefing papers.

Bob Cole had no specific assignments for today. But he did have a good relationship with Senator Long, as, of course, did Tommy Boggs and his firm. I found Cole huddled with Foster, chewing over the best arguments to make with the senator. "He's been around a long while," Bill was saying, "but he's still sharp on issues involving the state as well as taxation."

Cole nodded agreement, then raised the key concern: "Do you think our group has the muscle to overcome John Camp's personal ties to Long?"

"That's the jackpot question," admitted Foster. "But there are a couple of other factors that should be in our favor. Senator Long is close to Senator Johnston, and then too, as a fellow high-ranking member of a committee, Long may be disposed to defer to Senator McClure's wishes on this one, everything else being equal."

"Then it's up to us to make damn sure everything else *is* equal, in his mind," I piped in, thinking that this really should be one where we call in Tommy Boggs.

CHAPTER TWELVE

HAVING AN IMPACT

MARCH 24 -- THE FIRST Four, sans Bill Foster, had met for breakfast to chew over Texaco's response to the changes drawn up by Johnston, McClure and Ford. As far as we could tell, our opponent was staying with the argument they had made from the start. They had almost certainly hoped for language that would hurt the intrastate gas distributors, but the new wording was aimed at denying them that talking point.

Now, Cole, Dale, Ferguson and I were sitting close together at the bi-weekly meeting of the NAM Energy Committee. Chairman Jim Rubin was skimming through the myriad provisions of S. 615/H.R. 1517, and discussing what he thought could be further changes to the wording along the way. When he came to Section 316, the four of us looked at each other but said nothing.

Rubin shot a glance at me, and then at Texaco's Don Annett, again seated beside John Camp, and asked pointedly, "Anybody care to speak up on this language?" Annett smiled over at our group, we returned the smile, and still nobody spoke. So Rubin filled the void: "Well, I know that at least one group has been all over the Hill working this part of the bill." I tried to keep a blank face and look innocent, while Annett seemed a bit uneasy.

"Guys," Rubin pleaded, "This is a good piece of legislation. Let's not do anything to screw it up, *please*."

Now it was Annett's turn to smile. Camp, at his side, kept a poker face, while several others in the room seemed puzzled at the little sideshow, and Rubin pressed on with the next section in the legislation.

Later, walking out of the room, Lew Dale turned to the three of us and said softly, "Seems as if we're having an impact."

I had been mildly surprised at Rubin's comments until Cole reminded us, "Yeah, that seems clear. And I'd guess Annett's been bending his ear. Let's go chew over our next steps."

We decided to meet at the Georgia Pacific offices on I Street, NW.

* * *

After briefly reviewing the action so far, we opted to stay on the same course, and to pick up with our visits to the Senate Energy Committee members' offices over the next few days. We began by placing phone calls to the respective offices to set up the meetings.

As we were preparing to leave, I wondered aloud whether the other companies' retained counsel would get involved in this one, and if so, in what manner. The other three men figured there would be some reviewing of whatever language was being considered at every step in the legislative process. And Cole added, "I'm pretty sure there's a lot of exchange among all of our lawyers anyway, but you're right, we should make certain all our guys are aware of what's going on, and that they're not tripping over each other." I made a mental note to check in with Dick Packard and see if he and the general counsels for the other First Four companies were in touch with each other on this key issue.

The group also decided I should be the contact point between us and the other ad hoc group headed by Russell King and Rosemary O'Brien.

I left the meeting feeling that this issue was growing like wildfire on all fronts.

CHAPTER THIRTEEN

CONTRACT CARRIAGE

MARCH 28 -- I SPENT the morning in the offices of Senators Sam Nunn and John Heinz. John Ferguson had set up the Nunn staff visit after Ferguson had seen the staffer the first time, while I was joined by Lew Dale in the Heinz offices.

Nunn's legislative aide for energy issues mirrored the senator's quiet, studious personality. He listened carefully to our arguments, asked relevant questions about the position paper, and said he would wait to hear from Texaco before agreeing to set up a follow-up meeting for us with Nunn.

I double-checked, "So I take it Texaco hasn't been in to see you yet, right?"

"They've called for a visit and I'll see them next week."

Count Nunn's staff as undecided at this point. On to the Heinz offices in the Russell Senate Office Building.

* * *

Lew Dale and I knew most of the staffers for Senator Heinz. With both of our companies headquartered in Pennsylvania, and PPG having multiple facilities throughout the commonwealth -- especially in the western part of the state, and with Senator Heinz having formerly been a congressman from Pittsburgh -- my visits to the office had been fairly frequent.

John Heinz's legislative aide for energy issues was George Tenet (yes, the same George Tenet who later went on to work at the White House and become Director of the CIA). He listened to our position, nodded noncommittally and then raised the point we had expected.

"We'll need to be sure the proposed new version of the Energy Committee bill protects the local distribution companies in Pennsylvania. The language you guys are asking the committee to approve would cover intrastate gas only, and we just need to be sure our local distributors are safe, and that the contracts to bring natural gas to the consumer will be carried through.

That was the first time I had heard concerns about what was called "contract carriage." It would not be the last.

We showed Tenet the exemption for the local distribution companies, the so-called LDC's. He responded with, "Yes, but we'll still need to finetooth comb the wording to satisfy ourselves. I'm still not sure that having an exemption for this use of intrastate gas will protect our consumers. And, of course, I expect we'll be hearing from the other side on this issue."

Dale queried, "So what's a reasonable timeline for us to hear back from you and set up a meeting with the senator?"

"Give us a week, and we should be ready to move the ball."

In the hall outside Heinz's offices in the Russell Senate Office Building, Dale and I were uneasy about how the just-concluded meeting had gone. "Hell," Dale said, "you'd think with all our factories and labs in the state, the Heinz staff would be more clearly in our camp."

"We may be weeks, or longer, from a vote in committee," I responded. There's still lots of time for us to make the case with

Heinz, and if necessary, we can ask our CEO's to get involved as well. Since Texaco has their man working on it, we may want to do the same thing."

Dale jumped in immediately with, "Let's not use our trump card unless we absolutely have to, Ed. Our companies expect us to carry the ball on these issues."

"Agreed," I said. "But this is no ordinary issue, and while I have no idea how your chairman would react if asked to contact the senator, I'm pretty sure our guy Stan Williams is close to Heinz."

"Well, Dexter Baker, our president, might want to contact Heinz as well, but not just yet. I'd still figure Mr. Williams would not want to be used unless it's absolutely urgent," said Dale.

I was thinking that by now, Mr. Williams and all of PPG's top management had a pretty clear idea of the urgency of this case, but said only, "Well, you may be right about that. In any event, let's wait to see what the Heinz office has to say next week."

Dale and I went back to our own offices, where I called Patton Boggs to talk with Bill Foster.

"Well," I began, "today was not an overwhelming success. Neither Nunn's office nor Heinz's is ready to commit to us at this point, and Heinz's man says the senator's main concern is with contract carriage." Foster was fully familiar with that term. I replayed both visits and then added, "It's beginning to look like this one may be a squeaker in the Energy Committee."

"I'd expect that, Ed. In any event, we still have lots of work to do. I think it's time to set up a meeting of our group and Rosemary O'Brien's bunch, to run the traps and see where we all stand."

CHAPTER FOURTEEN

$3.4 BILLION

MARCH 29 -- AT JUST after 4 p.m., we filed into the conference room at Freeport McMoRan's Washington office, two floors above the PPG Industries offices. Russell King of Freeport and Rosemary O'Brien greeted us and introduced us to the people representing the other companies involved in the issue.

"Good to have our partners in crime here with us," King began.

"I prefer to think of us as fellow ministers doing the Lord's work on the Hill," offered Cole with a smile.

The others in the room, in addition to King and O'Brien, included George White, Bill Simpson for First Mississippi and Mississippi Chemical, Mike Nemeroff, a consultant representing Borden Chemical, and two outside attorneys, Christina Fleps and Jim Wilderotter. Fleps was on retainer to CF Industries, while Wilderotter worked with LP&L.

We spent the next hour and a half exchanging information about the impact of the original language in the Senate bill on our companies, and reviewing the members of the Energy Committee in whose states we had facilities. As it turned out, the total impact on the ten companies involved was roughly $3.4 billion. It was at this meeting that I finally learned that the bite on Air Products would be some two hundred fifty million if Texaco succeeded.

After Dale, Ferguson, Foster and I listed the committee members' offices we had visited, Russell King told us that the "Second Six" – as I came to call the group – had settled on their assignments, many of them overlapping our group's work. After an hour and ten minutes, the breakout of who would see whom showed that between us, the two groups were covering every committee member except Levin of Michigan, Weicker of Connecticut and Hawaii's Matsunaga.

And the Second Six also had discussed plans for a group visit to Senator Long as an obvious power player in anything affecting Louisiana. Lastly, they would also touch base with our champion, Senator Johnston, just to say thanks.

So we had added half a dozen companies to the fray, and several more committee members, bringing us up to 19 of the 22 senators in all. The group would also keep in close touch with committee staffers for both the majority and minority side, with specific assignments for those visits to be decided in the next few days. As for the House, the Second Six would brief us on their assignments at our next joint meeting.

"All right, people, let's go do the halls and walls routine," said King.

"Right, floors and doors," added Ferguson with a somewhat uncharacteristic flash of humor.

I found it interesting that the other outside attorneys in the room, including Wilderotter and Fleps though not Simpson, were highly deferential to Bill Foster's suggestions in determining who would take the lead in a few of these meetings and who would work most closely with the staff for Sens. Johnston and McClure. I ascribed Simpson's silence to the fact that he was by far the senior person in the meeting and felt no need to speak up at this point. With his white hair, wrinkled skin and raspy drawl, Bill Simpson looked to be well into his 60's if not older, and his roots with the Mississippi delegation to Congress were both deep and rock solid. That meant we could reasonably expect to have Senator Cochran's support. Some time later, King told me he and some of the others referred to Simpson as "Old Man River" because, "He just keeps rollin' along, and there's nothin' that's likely to stop him."

CHAPTER FIFTEEN

THE VOICE OF DOOM

MARCH 31 --THE INVOICE from Patton, Boggs and Blow was in the morning mail. These guys don't let any moss grow under their feet, I thought, as I opened the envelope. A copy had been sent to Bob Steder.

My immediate reaction was that PB&B's fee seemed steep for only 23 days. Then I remembered Dick Packard advising me to watch the billings "like a hawk." I examined the bill and saw a fairly lengthy list of attorneys -- senior and junior -- plus paralegals who were listed as having worked on the matter. I pored over each entry and had the feeling that at least a few of the charges seemed to cover duplicative work.

Then too, there was the matter of parceling out the one-fourth payment notices to Cole, Dale and Ferguson. Given his thirty thousand dollar limit, Cole would be especially concerned. After all, this legislation might well drag on through at least the first session of the 98th Congress and into 1984. Still, this was the first time I had worked with Patton Boggs, the generally acknowledged king of the Washington lobbying law firms.

As I pondered how best to approach the problem, the phone rang.

DODGING THE BULLET

It was Bill Harris, the VP and general manager of PPG's Chemical Division. After his first comment to me, I thought, how ironic and inconvenient that he should call at this moment.

The gravel-throated Harris and I were casual acquaintances. We had met a few times at various company meetings and had once played in the same foursome at a charity golf tournament. We were on a first-name basis. Or so I thought when I answered the phone.

"Jaffee," came the rasp, "this is Harris."

I recognized the voice and replied, "Yes, Bill."

"Jaffee, I was just handed a copy of the invoice from this Boggs firm. It's a hell of a lot of money for such a short time."

"Well, Bill, I agree with you. But remember that Tommy Boggs did basically get us Senator Johnston, who's a key player if not the most important one to have with us."

Harris ignored this last comment. "Jaffee, how much money is this Boggs firm gonna *cost* us?"

"Well, Bill, there're three other companies splitting the fee (I chose not to mention the $30,000 limit set by one of them). Let's see, it'll likely take at least 14 months……"

"*Dammit*, Jaffee! I didn't ask how *long*, I asked how *much*!"

That's when it occurred to me that Harris might have been working on the Chemical Division budget when he saw the invoice. After a slight pause, I responded: "I figure our share will come to about $75,000."

"That's a lot of *money*, Jaffee."

To this day I don't know what prompted my response, but I said, "Bill -- *sir* -- let me ask you one thing. Would you spend seventy-five cents to save three hundred dollars?"

"Of *course* I would!"

"Then you'll spend seventy-five thousand to save three hundred million, right?"

I was hoping to hell my math was right, but in any event, Harris apparently wasn't looking for a calculator. There was a pause of about five seconds, during which I saw my career circling the drain.

The gravelly voice finally came back, with just three words, followed by the phone slamming down: *"Just... don't... lose!"*

* * *

I couldn't pull back the exact source of the quote, but at the next meeting of our group, in PPG's conference room, there was a sign on the wall: "The knowledge that one is to be executed in a fortnight wonderfully focuses the mind."

CHAPTER SIXTEEN

"REMEMBER, THEY WORK FOR US"

MARCH 31 -- WITH A bit of trepidation, I phoned Bill Foster.

"Thanks for the speed in getting your invoice over to us," I began. "But I have to say I was surprised at the amount of the bill."

Foster was immediately on the defensive. "Ed, this month was front-loaded to a degree. There were several meetings with your folks, plus the four conferences among our own attorneys that you see listed, and then there were my Hill visits. And we did bring Bennett on board right from the start, and that alone should help get us a bunch of other members of the committee."

I opted not to remind Foster that in the end, it was George White who got us Senator Johnston, although Tommy Boggs' quick action did set up the meeting, and it was Foster and Boggs who invited White. Instead, I replied that "It looks as if there was some duplicative work by members of the firm." As examples, I mentioned listings for time spent researching the same point in three instances.

Faced with a palpable chill from the other end of the line, it was time to make a specific request. I suggested, "It would definitely make things easier, not just for me but for all four of our companies, if you could bring this first bill down a bit."

"I'll see what we can do, okay?" Foster responded with an edge in his voice. There was no thought of small talk after that, and the conversation ended quickly.

I phoned Bob Steder and reviewed the call to Foster. "So Bill Harris called you, I'm assuming" said Bob.

"Oh, yeah. Indeed he did, and as you must know, he was not exactly pleased."

"Well, you're still alive, so that's something. But look, Patton Boggs is working for *us* on this, so don't be shy in dealing with them."

"I know," I replied, "but it's not a comfortable feeling to realize that the working relationship with our major league lobbying law firm just got somewhat tense."

What I didn't see the need to share with Steder was that, contrary to the view most people have of lobbyists, my experience had virtually always been that the corporate reps I dealt with were hard-working, honorable men and women who did their best to represent their employers' interests in a decent and respectful way, without seeking out controversy. Yes, there were a few bad actors, but on the whole, these people were a good bunch to work with and to have on your side. And having a tense relationship with our power broker would not be a comfortable situation for any of us.

Instead, I said, "It's just that I was surprised by how much Foster seemed taken aback by what was really a simple request to lower their fee a bit. Anyway, we'll wait for the adjusted invoice before I send it out to the other three companies."

CHAPTER SEVENTEEN

"LET'S PUT THIS ONE IN THE BANK"

APRIL 11 -- SOMETIMES BREAKS come from a place you would least expect. Sitting at my desk at about 9:30 on the first morning after Easter recess, I had a phone call from Donald O'Hara, president of the National Petroleum Refiners Association.

I had met O'Hara once, years earlier, and then only briefly while interviewing him for a story in our company paper, PPG News, on organization and structure in the petroleum industry. But he asked if I were free to meet at his office. I asked why. He said only, "It involves the natural gas decontrol bill."

That was good enough for me. We set up the meeting for three that afternoon.

So word of the set-to between Texaco and our companies had become pretty much common knowledge in DC, or at least among those interested in energy legislation. I phoned Bob Steder to brief him and to get his take on what O'Hara might want.

"I've no idea," Steder allowed. "But let me do a quick check to see if I'm right in assuming Texaco's an NPRA member."

Bob called back in ten minutes to say that yes, Texaco was in the association.

"So," I said, "I'd assume they're behind O'Hara's call to me, and that there'll be some sort of pressure to get our group to back off, don't you think?"

"That seems logical," Bob responded. "And I assume O'Hara doesn't have the clout or close enough ties to Stan Williams or any of the other CEO's in the First Four to call them directly, so he's coming after you."

"My, how reassuring," I offered, and then added, "If I were Texaco, I'd be looking for a wedge issue that might put pressure on NPRA to try to stop us in some way," I said. "How about if I call Sara Schotland and sound her out?"

"Do it."

* * *

Schotland was her usual analytical self. "That's interesting," she began. "As you know, exploring for petroleum sometimes yields natural gas as well, and the two forms of energy can be different arms of the same corporation, as they are with Texaco. But you don't refine natural gas, you just put it in the pipeline, so the link is not that strong. No, it has to be something else, something more basic, more tactical, that's behind O'Hara's call to you. Just wish I knew what he's thinking."

I was going to brief the other three Washington reps anyway before seeing O'Hara, but Sara's comment made me think immediately of the key tactician in our group, Bob Cole. I thanked Sara and told her I'd check with both Cole and Bill Foster.

Both men had the same idea. As Cole put it, "Let's not overthink this thing. Remember that it's a huge piece of legislation, with sections that are bound to affect some refiners. Why not just listen to what O'Hara has to say?"

Bill Foster agreed. "Look, O'Hara invited you, and nobody else with you. Obviously, he's talked with NPRA's attorneys, but I'd be really surprised if he plans to have his legal eagles in the room. As long as you make no commitments, there's little downside to your meeting with the guy. But do keep me up to speed on how the meeting goes."

After those calls, I briefed Dale and Ferguson.

* * *

NPRA's offices on DeSales Street were one short block from the PPG Washington office. O'Hara, alone in the office, rose to greet me. He was about 5'11", medium build, with hair that was once black but was now almost all grey. He looked in his mid-60's.

We dispensed quickly with the pleasantries, and O'Hara sat behind his desk as I took a chair on the other side. That in itself seemed instructive, since most people who host a meeting will sit anywhere but behind the desk, to put the visitor more at ease. So I had the immediate impression that O'Hara was about to put a hard sell on me.

"Ed," he began, "as you no doubt know, Texaco is a member of NPRA. Their refining capacity is huge."

"I know," I replied. "They must be one of your largest members."

"Yes, but I was referring to their refining operations. Your concern, as I understand it, has to do with a totally different end of their business, their natural gas pipelines."

I paused before saying anything. Could it be that O'Hara was actually distancing NPRA from Texaco on this issue?

After a moment, I asked, "Don, let me be sure of what I think you're telling me. Are you saying that Texaco's natural gas operations are no concern of yours and NPRA's?"

Now it was O'Hara's turn to pause, before answering. After several seconds, he said, "Essentially, that's right. We support them completely in their refining concerns, but in this instance, it's out of our bailiwick."

"Okay," I rejoined. Thank you for clarifying that." I thought briefly of saying more, but -- remembering one of the basic rules of lobbying: "Once you've won, stop!" -- I merely added, "And thanks for asking me over to set the record straight. Anything else we should discuss?"

"Well, there is one thing I'd ask, Ed. Just see if you guys can keep from tanking the entire bill, okay?"

I grinned and nodded.

* * *

Smiling all the way back to my office, I tried to dispassionately analyze the impact on us of what had just happened in a remarkably brief meeting. Clearly, Texaco had leaned on O'Hara to try to put whatever pressure he could on our coalition. But if he was not going to cooperate with one of his largest members, then why bother to say anything to me? No, there still had to be more to it than that.

I phoned Steder immediately. He was as mystified as I about what had just taken place, but added, "Hell, if it's a gift, let's just take it and move on."

Bob Cole took a somewhat cloudier view of the meeting. "On the face of it, it's good news, of course. But my guess is there's gotta be something else involved for O'Hara to dismiss Texaco's request ... assuming we're right in thinking they leaned on him. My guess, and that's all it is, is that O'Hara ran Texaco's request past some of the other large members of NPRA and got a cool reception because those companies don't want to give Texaco a competitive advantage. On the other hand, if he's acting alone, the last thing we should be doing is to worry about his motives. Either way, let's put this one in the bank. I assume you'll bring Dale and Ferguson up to speed."

"Right away," I replied. "And Foster as well."

Not for the first time, Bill Foster basically echoed Bob Cole's thinking. "It's beginning to look as if the other big fish in the industry, and some of the smaller ones as well, may have put the word out that Texaco's pretty much on its own in this fight. No way to know for sure, but it's an assumption I'm comfortable with, aren't you?"

"You bet I am."

CHAPTER EIGHTEEN

WORKING THE HOUSE

APRIL 12, 9 A.M. -- WE GATHERED at the Air Products offices, without Foster, and, as Dale's administrative assistant poured the coffee, Lew said, "How about we check the list and see where we are with the Senate Energy Committee? Then we can begin thinking about assignments with House Energy and Commerce."

"Before we start," I said, "I have the initial bill from Patton Boggs. I spoke with Foster and got them to bring it down by about four thousand." I distributed each company's invoice.

"They don't come cheap, that's for sure," said Ferguson. The other two were silent, so I added, "I've sent our bill on to Pittsburgh. If the rest of you could have your share of the bill paid as soon as possible, it would help keep things on an even keel with Foster. I realize the Boggs firm is working for us, but we do want them fully involved."

"I'm not sure I follow you," said Dale.

"It's just that Bill Foster is a star in the firm," I answered. "He's already a partner, and we need him to stay committed to us and to this issue."

"Wait a minute, Ed." It was Cole. "Just how tense was your discussion with Foster?"

"Not tense at all on my part, Bob. But Foster got all defensive, and when I somewhat gingerly pressed the issue, he obviously wasn't pleased. I imagine the Boggs firm isn't used to having its invoices questioned."

"Well, look," offered Cole, "You're our point man with the guy, and we're depending on you to keep him, and the firm, in line. How you do that is up to you. Just do it."

I nodded, deciding not to remind Cole that I was concerned about his company's $30,000 cap; obviously they shared the same concern.

* * *

With that, we turned to the main reason for the meeting. The agenda included reports on further meetings with staffers for members of the Senate Energy Committee, a report from Cole on his latest conversation with committee staffer Daryl Owen and a first look at the House Energy and Commerce Committee, beginning with the Fossil and Synthetic Fuels Subcommittee.

Cole gave us Owen's report that Chairman McClure had not yet begun to push other members of the Senate Energy Committee to buy into the revised language in the bill. "Any idea how soon the chairman plans to move on lining up his fellow members?" Dale asked.

"Not yet, Lew," replied Cole, "He might just be waiting to see how well we're doing with our visits before twisting any arms. Or maybe not. In any case, we'll know soon enough."

We reviewed where we stood based on our earlier visits, and decided that it was time to ask for meetings with Senators Nunn, Bentsen and Heinz, and also with Bumpers, to affirm his agreement to go along with the committee chair and ranking member. We would also meet with Washington State's Senator Jackson, if "Scoop" Jackson had recovered from his illness. We would use the arguments in our earlier position paper plus the Texaco testimony from 1977 in Louisiana and Sara Schotland's point paper. The visits would be made by the same men who had spoken earlier with the senators' staff, except for the Nunn visit. That would be a group effort, including Cole and Dale in addition to Ferguson and me. Sam Nunn was a widely respected moderate-to-conservative Democrat who often kept his positions close to the vest until voting time was near. We wanted to make it clear to him that quite a few companies -- some with operations in Georgia -- and their employees would be hurt by the language in the original bill, and to see if he would oppose Texaco's attempt to reinstate that language.

At the same time, Bob Cole would touch base again with Daryl Owen of the Energy Committee staff, and I would ask Bill Foster to get further feedback from Johnston staffer Betsy Moeller.

* * *

Once the Senate Energy Committee assignments were settled, we turned to the 42-member House Energy and Commerce Committee, and to its Fossil and Synthetic Fuels Subcommittee, the group to which the House version of the bill was first sent. Our strategy in the House would, of course, be the opposite of what we were doing in the Senate, since Texaco's language had not been deleted from H.R. 1517. Our goal was to have our language from the new Senate version of the bill picked up in the House version.

The full committee chairman was Rep. John Dingell, a 28-year member from Michigan whose power was such that he was generally known throughout Capitol Hill as "Mr. Chairman."

With the Democrats holding the majority in the House, Dingell ruled the Energy and Commerce Committee with an iron hand. His subcommittee chairmen had sway over their panels, but Dingell managed to be assigned ex-officio to whatever subcommittee he chose.

More than once, I had seen Dingell lock swords with, and tie up, the Environment Subcommittee, chaired by Rep. Henry Waxman of California. Dingell would sit in the far left seat of the subcommittee room, as viewed from the audience. He would wait his turn to speak and then pepper the chairman with countless questions. I sometimes wondered at the fact that following a heated exchange between the two, they would walk off seeming to chat amiably with each other. Then again, it would never pay to show true animus to Chairman Dingell.

In our situation, the legislation, H.R. 1517, would go first to the Fossil and Synthetic Fuels Subcommittee, chaired by Democratic Rep. Phil Sharp of Indiana, so that's where we placed our initial emphasis. (*The party in control of the House or Senate always chairs every subcommittee as well as each full committee.*) Sharp was a gentlemanly moderate Democrat who would listen to all sides of an argument and then listen to his staff before taking a position. At the same time, as with all members of Congress, he was carefully tuned to the desires of his constituency. So everything else being equal -- which, of course, was not always the case -- he might favor a well-prepared and well-presented argument.

It was apparent that the coming weeks would be far busier than we had anticipated.

CHAPTER NINETEEN

"SWINGING FOR THE FENCES"

APRIL 13, 9:10 A.M. -- AS IT happened, we had less time than anticipated to meet with members of Rep. Sharp's subcommittee. Shortly after the end of our meeting the day before, I had a call from Bill Foster alerting me to the fact that the Fossil and Synthetic Fuels Subcommittee of House Energy and Commerce had just decided to hold hearing on the 15th. That signaled that our group should accelerate our meetings with the subcommittee members.

After alerting Bob Steder, I arranged for a conference call at 1 p.m. with the rest of the "First Four" and the "Second Six," and then called Foster back to ask if he could possibly line up a witness for our side of the issue on the committee hearing docket for the 15th. Foster said, "This is really unusually short notice, but I'll see if we can do it. And Ed, that means putting several of our staff to work preparing the testimony."

"I realize that, Bill, but as you know, we have to roll with the punches." Meanwhile, I was wondering what Bill Harris would say when he saw the next month's invoice.

My first assignment was with Rep. Doug Walgren, a member of Phil Sharp's subcommittee and a moderate Democrat who represented part of Pittsburgh and much of the surrounding area. That encompassed several PPG labs and some of our smaller manufacturing plants, some nine locations in all. The previous fall, I had squired Walgren on a tour of the environmental facilities at several of those locations and had set up a meeting for him at corporate headquarters with the environmental quality leaders from within all four of PPG's operating divisions.

I had visited with Walgren perhaps fifteen times on a variety of subjects, and his legislative assistant for energy issues, Mary Jo Zacchero, and I had become friendly. Mary Jo, dark-haired, with a medium build and about five foot four, was a tireless worker with a good sense of humor. When I phoned her to explain why "I really need to meet with the boss this morning if at all possible," she put me on hold, spoke with Walgren's chief of staff, Jon Delano, and told me to get over there within the hour. I assumed she also briefed the appointments secretary.

I then called Bob Cole and asked if he would like to join me in meeting with Walgren; he said he could shift a couple of other things on his schedule and would meet me at Walgren's office in the Rayburn House Office Building. Cole was familiar with full committee chairman Dingell as well as the House leadership in both parties.

* * *

Cole and I entered Doug Walgren's office at a little after 11 a.m. Mary Jo Zacchero came in with us. As we moved to the small conference table in his inner office, Walgren, a Dartmouth graduate with a Stanford law degree, had a legal pad and a pen, ready to take notes. "What's the urgent problem?" he asked. I went through the impact of the issue on PPG, briefed him on the others in our coalition and brought him up to date on what we had done so far in the Senate and on our now-expedited plans to meet with House subcommittee members.

I asked, "Any idea when Chairman Sharp plans to go to markup on H.R. 1517?" Mary Jo interjected that the bill number was now HR-1760, and that the subcommittee staff had just finished making changes before reissuing it as a "staff draft," a not-uncommon practice with major legislation in either house of Congress. In this case, it was a clear indication that all sorts of people with a wide range of interests were seeking input to the wording in various sections of the bill, and that some of what they wanted had been added in the staff draft.

Walgren said he would let us know about markup as soon as he got word from the chairman's office.

Turning to Mary Jo, I asked, "I guess you haven't yet found out about possible changes to the provisions covering first sale, direct sale, not-for-resale natural gas, right?"

"Ed," she replied, "I didn't even know until just now that there was anything about that in the bill, or that you had a problem with that issue."

"Right, of course. Sorry," I replied.

Walgren took notes as Cole and I made our case, and asked several pointed, pertinent questions, many of them the same arguments Texaco had been making, including their key position that our four companies were getting an unfair price advantage compared with other companies in the state. We countered each of his points, and he finally put down his pen and said, "All right; you've convinced me. Now go convince the others on the subcommittee to carry your amendment."

Encouraged by Walgren's response, I took the opportunity to ask if he would sponsor the amendment to H.R. 1760 for us. "It's a bit early for that," he replied. "Tomorrow is just hearings. Let's see how things look before we talk about legislative fixes." Then he added, "I'd like to protect PPG if that's doable." I nodded.

Walgren also asked if we had a witness for the upcoming hearings. I replied that Patton Boggs was working on that at this moment. On hearing the name of our law firm, Doug offered a slight smile, and said, "Tommy Boggs, eh? You guys are swinging for the fences."

I couldn't resist saying, "And you're one of our key hitters."

"So go talk to the other members of the subcommittee," came the reply. "And keep Mary Jo posted."

CHAPTER TWENTY

SHIFTING INTO HIGH GEAR

APRIL 14 -- THINGS WERE heating up faster than I expected. The phone was ringing as I walked into the PPG offices at 7:55 a.m. It was Foster calling with a heads-up that the Senate Energy and Commerce Committee planned to go straight to full committee markup, skipping the subcommittee stage entirely, a surprise to me. The session was scheduled for May 4, leaving us just twenty days to try to convince a majority of the committee of the validity of our case.

"So, do you think Texaco's behind this?" I asked.

"Maybe. Or maybe it's just a busy committee schedule and they want to get this thing out of the way. Either way, we need to step it up and be ready."

Foster also reported that given the unexpected bump-up in the committee markup calendar, he and Tommy Boggs felt it would be more valuable to us if they skipped the House subcommittee hearing testimony tomorrow -- "One of our paralegals will attend and report back to us" -- and got moving on meetings with senators. My initial feeling was that Foster was right; there was limited time for all of us to shift into high gear. And at the same time, I was relieved in knowing that not having the Boggs firm working further in preparing our testimony would save us a bundle in billings. I briefed Foster on our success with Walgren.

I then made several calls, the first to alert Mary Jo Zacchero about our change in plans for the Sharp subcommittee hearings. Next, I called Bob Steder to brief him on this latest news as well as letting him know we had Doug Walgren in our camp and that he might be willing to carry our amendment in Phil Sharp's subcommittee.

Steder was pleased to know Walgren was with us but was more worried about the Senate, and he wondered how we were going to line up at least eleven members of the Senate Energy Committee in short order. If all 22 members showed up for the committee markup, we would need at least 11 votes in order to defeat the anticipated Texaco amendment. Since Texaco needed twelve votes to carry it, we would win in a tie vote. I replied that all ten companies plus Patton Boggs and the law firms for some of the others in our ad hoc coalition would be involved.

Bob's answer: "Make sure you stay on top of it, and keep me posted, please."

The next calls went to Russell King and Rosemary O'Brien. Turned out that both of them had already heard about the cancelled subcommittee hearing from their own sources, and were setting up a meeting of the "Second Six" companies for that afternoon to plan their Senate and House assignments. I told them that our four companies would do the same thing and suggested we meet again as a full group the next day.

They agreed, and King added that he thought he, O'Brien and Bill Simpson were already close to getting Sen. Bumpers' vote.

After that, I updated Cole, Ferguson, Dale and Bill Foster by conference call and set up a session in our offices for 2 p.m.

* * *

Lew Dale started our meeting by suggesting it was time for me to join him in going back to Sen. Heinz's office, only this time to see the senator himself. I quickly agreed, and the group went on to plan follow-up meetings -- based on assignments the First Four had carried out earlier and including Bill Foster -- with members of the Senate Energy Committee. For meetings involving George White, we decided to wait until tomorrow's joint sit-down with the Second Six and their attorneys. After our Senate Energy Committee meetings were assigned we would turn to the House and Rep. Sharp's subcommittee.

So as before, and in addition to Sen. Heinz, I was to see Sens. Bentsen and Nickles, and join in the group meeting with Nunn. As for Sen. Johnston, Foster would stay in close contact with him, and both Foster and Cole would stay close to the committee staff, both Republican and Democratic.

Ferguson would see Sens. Bumpers and Jackson, and take part in the group meeting with Sen. Nunn. Bob Cole would see Sen. Warner of Virginia.

And also, from our team, Foster would have the lead in seeing Sen. Johnston and staff, and would join me in the Bentsen visit as well as seeing Sens. Bradley and McClure. All four of us understood that if necessary, Tommy Boggs could be called in on selected visits, most notably with Chairman McClure, to make sure we would have no surprise change of course by the committee chairman.

I couldn't escape the feeling that, in a sense, we were going into a military-style battle in short order, and on two fronts, in the Senate and House. Given the size of our 10-company team and the platoon of lawyers in our camp, and given the seeming antipathy of the National Petroleum Refiners Association to the Texaco position, it would seem we were well armed .

But we had no reading on the position of by far the largest trade association in Texaco's field, the American Petroleum Institute, a group with enormous political clout. And, I reminded myself, even leaving API aside, Texaco was a formidable opponent in any lobbying battle. I made a mental note to find time to nose quietly around in the next couple of days with an acquaintance from the community of oil company Washington representatives.

It was time to look at our lobbying assignments with the House subcommittee members. Even though Senate Energy was our immediate priority, with Sharp's subcommittee markup following Senate Energy markup, we wanted to have an indication of which companies in the "First Four" would see which members of the full House committee as well as the subcommittee, and to be ready to move on those visits on short notice.

Our goal was still to get support for an amendment that would add the same wording Senators Johnston, McClure and Ford had inserted in the Senate version of the legislation. Our thinking was that having the same language in both the House and Senate versions would drastically simplify things when the Senate and House conferees got together to iron out differences in the two bills after both houses of Congress had passed them. Bill Foster had already gained approval from our champion, Senator Johnston, for that approach.

There were ten Democrats and eight Republicans on Phil Sharp's subcommittee. Taking into account that members of the "Second Six" might overlap some of our assignments, we broke out our visits as follows:

On the majority side: Chairman Phil Sharp (D-IN) - Foster (with the possibility of Tommy Boggs, if necessary) and Cole;

Rep. Paul Rogers (D-FL) - Jaffee (I had worked with his staff on environmental issues). We hoped George White would also plan a visit;

Rep. Tim Wirth (D-CO) - We would leave this one to Rosemary O'Brien;

Rep. Ed Markey (D-MA) - Nobody had facilities in his district, but Bob Cole volunteered, pointing out that Markey was on record strongly opposing the power and reach of the petroleum companies;

Al Swift (D-WA) - Ferguson;

Tom Luken (D-OH) - Jaffee;

Al Gore (D-TN) – Cole said he would ask O'Brien to join him in the visit;

Mickey Leland (D-TX) and Mike Synar (D-OK) – While we knew our chances of gaining their support were slim, Cole and I agreed to take a shot, as time allowed;

That left Doug Walgren, and I had already planned to get back to Mary Jo Zacchero after our joint session with the Second Six tomorrow.

On the minority side: Ralph Hall (R-TX), the ranking member of the full Energy and Commerce Committee -- We basically wrote him off as a supporter, with the understanding that if time allowed, I might make a quick stop by the office, and that we would ask O'Brien if she was interested in doing the same thing.

Wayne Dowdy (R-MS) – We would leave this visit to Bill Simpson;

Ranking subcommittee member Jim Broyhill (R-NC) – Jaffee (We had a large fiber glass plant in his district, and I had visited with the congressman several times on other issues);

Rep. Ed Madigan (R-IL) – Jaffee, due to our flat glass manufacturing plant in his district, and O'Brien might join us on this visit as well;

Tom Corcoran (R-IL) – Jaffee, with PPG's Phil Pulizzi, who knew Corcoran well;

Jim Slattery (D-KS) -- Foster, who figured O'Brien would also want to see Slattery, since Kansas was in the heart of CF Industries' agricultural areas of interest;

Rep. Mike Oxley (R-OH) – Jaffee, with Gary Wilson of PPG's Washington office. Wilson and Oxley had been fraternity brothers in college;

Don Ritter (R-PA) – Jaffee, since PPG had a small presence in his district;

Then there was Rep. Billy Tauzin, on the full Energy and Commerce Committee though not on the Sharp subcommittee. Tauzin was obviously a special case, given his support for Texaco ten years earlier when he was in the Louisiana legislature. Bob Cole took the assignment, since Kaiser's major Louisiana facility was in Tauzin's district. Lew Dale volunteered to join in the visit. We anticipated George White wanting to see Tauzin as well. I asked Foster what he thought of also having Tommy Boggs ask his mother Lindy to contact Tauzin.

"We'd rather not bring Rep. Boggs into it, though I realize she could be helpful," replied Foster, adding that while members of the state's congressional delegation often did favors for one another, Lindy Boggs knew full well that Tauzin had been point man for Texaco a decade ago.

"One more point," I added, to the group. "As Bill Foster pointed out to me when we retained Patton Boggs, their of counsel attorney is Bill O'Hara, a former Michigan congressman, no relation to NPRA's Don O'Hara. Do you think we can use him with these House members?"

Foster answered. "I'll check and see if he's tight with any of these guys, and let you know. And in any event, we'll sound him out about weighing in with Chairman Dingell in full committee and with several House members when the bill reaches the floor."

"Tomorrow's meeting of our two groups will be busy," I offered, "and then the real fun starts."

CHAPTER TWENTY-ONE

"I COULD NOSE ABOUT QUIETLY"

APRIL 15, 8:30 A. M. -- BILL FOSTER was on the line, telling me that staffers for Phil Sharp had raised a possible red flag. "Sharp seems less than pleased with the way things are moving on the bill."

"Meaning what?" I asked.

"Well, the word from his staff is that the chairman feels the bill still needs a lot of work, and especially in terms of protecting the public consumer of natural gas."

"But won't our language take care of that problem for him, at least at the intrastate level?"

"You'd think so," answered Foster. "But it seems Sharp is making that concern the *sine qua non* for his moving on the bill. And, of course, he may be talking about other sections of the bill as well."

"Damn! Then we've gotta get to him ASAP, don't you think?"

"I do. And since Walgren's in our camp, why not use him as well, to get the word to Sharp?"

"I'll call Mary Jo Zacchero in his office right away and see if we can set that up."

* * *

Five minutes later -- Mary Jo was in a meeting when I called, so I explained the situation to Jon Delano, Walgren's staff chief, and asked him to, "Ask M.J. if she can please get back to me soon on this."

I left a message for Foster, who had stepped out of the office. That done, there was still an hour before the meeting of our combined groups was to begin. It was time to do a bit of sleuthing with one of my oil company brethren in the Washington representative community. It appeared that virtually every oil company was a member of the American Petroleum Institute. I didn't want to question any of the senior people in the Washington offices of the companies I called, lest they choose to contact Don Annett at Texaco. But I was friendly enough with some of the other reps that I felt I could sound out one of them.

I called Ralph Zaaenga with Phillips Petroleum, a large, gentle man who had shared a Kennedy Center concert with my wife and me a month earlier.

"Ralph," I began, "It's Ed Jaffee."

"Hey, Ed, calling about another evening outing with Elspeth and me?"

"Well, that's not a bad idea, and I know Sharon would like it. But actually, I need a bit of information, if it's not too much to ask."

"I'll help if I can. Whaddya need?"

"Well, you may or may not know that Texaco is in a squabble with PPG and some other companies about some language in the president's natural gas decontrol bill."

"That's hardly news, Ed. I've heard my people here talking about it."

"Oh, really? What's the word from them, if you don't mind my asking?"

"Well, pretty much it's that this is Texaco's issue. We have plenty to keep us busy without getting involved in their battles."

I was so relieved to hear Ralph's answer that I almost ended the conversation without pursuing the real reason for the call. After a moment I said, "Well, that's good to know. And it'd be still more important if I knew whether API plans to weigh in on the issue."

There was the briefest of pauses before Zaaenga said, "I guess I could nose about quietly. You know ... see what's on their lobbying agenda and let you know."

"Ralph, you've read my mind. I'd be grateful if you could do that. Meanwhile, my best to Elspeth, and let's do think about another evening on the town."

* * *

I walked up the two flights to Freeport McMoRan's offices for the joint session between our two ad hoc groups. Bill Foster was coming down the hall as I opened the stairwell door. I quickly briefed him on my call to Walgren's office, and we walked into the meeting together.

Rosemary O'Brien led off the discussion by reaffirming the Senate Energy lobbying assignments for the Second Six, with no changes from the earlier schedule. She then added that George White had done a little extra-curricular work, in seeing Senator Lawton Chiles of Florida.

White relayed that we could count on Chiles' vote on the floor. I nodded and said, "That's extra credit, thinking ahead to floor action as well as your work with committee members," then added, "I suspect Brother Simpson has had good results in seeing Senator Cochran as well."

Simpson responded, "Well, mistuh cha-uh-mun, ah think we can put Senatuh Cochran in ow-uh cay-ump." I offered a surprised smile at

Simpson's reference to me, and replied, "That's good work, and just call me Mr. Facilitator."

King had already met with Senators Bentsen, Nickles and Bumpers, joining George White on that last visit. He reported that while it looked as if Bumpers was now with us, he had had little or no luck with Bentsen or Nickles. No surprise on those last two and I made a mental note to tell the others in the First Four that given our time constraints, and unless they felt strongly to the contrary, I'd say we should write off Nickles and Bentsen.

The rest of the Second Six reported in as well. In a surprise, Mike Nemeroff, representing Borden, said he had already visited with Sen. Metzenbaum's staff and that they had said the senator might want to support us. I would call his staff first thing in the morning to arrange a follow-up visit.

The group was waiting for word from John Ferguson before setting up a meeting with Senator Nunn. Ferguson spoke up. "I'll call the senator's office this afternoon and set up the meeting. How many of you would like to take part?" White volunteered, and Ferguson said, "Good. George, Ed and I will be at that one."

Lew Dale added that he and I planned to see Senator Heinz as soon as possible.

Bill Foster said he hadn't had a chance to speak with Senator Stevens but would make the call "later today," adding that Tommy Boggs might join him on that visit.

And again, I found myself playing the scorecard game, with the same troubling tally; it was clearly too close to call in the Senate Energy and Natural Resources Committee.

Jim Wilderotter, the outside attorney for LP&L, then spoke up. "What's the situation with that possible group visit with Senator Long?"

"Yeah," Foster replied, "about that. I spoke with Tommy and he thinks it's best for us to leave that up to Bennett Johnston. He's Long's junior senator in the state and knows him as well as or better than anyone else. When we first discussed a group visit at that earlier meeting, I probably should've suggested we wait to see what Tommy and Lindy Boggs thought, but now we know their druthers. If anybody can offset the influence of John Camp as Russell's personal attorney, it's Bennett. And Bennett might be able to set up a joint meeting among McClure, Long and himself."

Nobody disagreed, so I nodded to Foster and he reported on what he had heard from the subcommittee staff about the chairman's concern over protection of the interstate consumer, since our language dealt only with intrastate natural gas. Foster also noted that, in theory at least, decontrolling natural gas should increase the supply and thus lower prices for all gas. "At least that's the theory," he reasoned.

I said that I planned to meet with Doug Walgren as soon as possible to see if he would help us out with the chairman.

Several in the room showed concern at Foster's report, and I assured them that Walgren was both firmly with us and that he was fairly close with Sharp. Wilderotter wondered if any of their group should also try to see Sharp, but Russell King, as a former Senate legislative aide, countered that it was "always best for a member of the committee to speak first with the chairman. Just let us know how Walgren does with Sharp, and we can follow up then."

With that, the meeting ended. It had been a productive session, and the First Four's task had been clarified somewhat as a result of the pro-and-con feedback from the Second Six.

CHAPTER TWENTY-TWO

"THAT'S NOT GONNA HAPPEN"

APRIL 18, 3:30 P.M. -- TENA BUZZED me to say Bill Foster was on the phone.

"Ed," he began, "you'll recall that I said our group needs to keep tabs on what the Department of Energy and the White House might be thinking about our lobbying efforts. I've just spoken with Danny Boggs, no relation to Tommy. He's Deputy Secretary of Energy, and though he was noncommittal on the matter, I'm almost certain we have a problem with him. I took the liberty of asking for a meeting, to include the First Four, and he agreed to meet with us next week, on the 22nd at 10 a.m. Can you make it, and will you contact the others?"

I had no meetings yet locked in for the 22nd, so I quickly agreed on both counts, and then added, "What did he say that makes you uneasy?"

"He emphasized what he called the critical importance of this legislation to the president and to DOE Secretary Don Hodel, and then added that they would like to see the bill come out with as few changes as possible."

"Well hell," I rejoined, "that's nothing new. Everybody wants the bills they introduce to go through cleanly, and your paralegal reported that they said the same thing at the Sharp subcommittee hearing. But Boggs certainly knows that's not gonna happen."

"Right," replied Foster. "And I know there've been literally dozens, if not hundreds, of changes in other parts of the legislation. But we still need to know how locked-in the administration is on this one."

"Okay, I'll call the other three guys. So let's see; we're juggling upcoming action in the Sharp subcommittee, the full Senate Energy Committee and now DOE's concerns."

"This just gets to be more and more fun," Foster concluded dryly.

CHAPTER TWENTY-THREE

"PHILOSOPHICALLY OPPOSED"

APRIL 19, 9:10 A.M. -- LEW DALE was on the phone with me.

"Ed, I just spoke with George Tenet in Heinz's office. He checked the appointments secretary and says we can meet with the senator today at two if you're free."

"Let's do it. It'll be good to talk to the head man this time. But I'll have to leave word as to where and when I can be reached by Walgren if he or Mary Jo calls back while I'm out."

* * *

Tenet was waiting for us when we entered the Heinz suite of offices. "Guys, I'm really sorry, but the senator got called away to an unexpected meeting."

"Damn," I blurted. "When do you expect him back?"

"I'm not sure. Could be a long one."

"Just to be sure," asked Dale, "he does realize this is an issue of major concern to two large employers in the state?"

"He knows," came the reply, with what I took to be a bit of an edge in the voice.

"Well, look," I said, "time's drawing short for action on this bill, so if we leave you the materials we were gonna discuss with Senator Heinz, will you make certain he has the chance to review everything and that he'll get back to us with his position on the issue?"

"Yes. And I can tell you that the senator is philosophically opposed to contract abrogation. But I also know he's not pleased with the way McClure, Johnston and Ford have redrafted the overall bill."

This last comment surprised me. "Well, George," I responded, "we both know that several other members of the committee, including Republicans, are using Johnston's support for the new language as leverage to gain inclusion in the markup vehicle for points they consider vital."

"That's no surprise. It always works that way," said Tenet.

"Then what's the problem?" asked Dale.

"The senator just is displeased with the way this has been done."

I held my tongue rather than saying something dangerously stupid, like that Senator Heinz had certainly been around long enough to know how legislative compromises are forged. Instead, I shook my head barely perceptibly.

"Then I guess that's the best we can do at this point," said Dale.

We gave Tenet the full packet of briefing papers, including Sara Schotland's analysis and the Texaco testimony to the Louisiana officials, as well as Foster's paper on sanctity of contract. He reviewed that paper and nodded, but said nothing.

We reiterated the arguments we had made in our earlier visit with Tenet. Finally, I asked him again to let us know what Senator Heinz had to say after reading our materials, including the Schotland paper.

"I'll do that."

* * *

In the hall outside the offices, both Dale and I were worried. "I think Tenet's hiding something, something else in the bill that bothers Heinz," offered Lew.

"Let's give Heinz the benefit of the doubt," I said. "Let's accept that he's locked into a meeting. Still, I don't get a good feeling."

"Me either," replied Dale. "The man's a key vote, for our two companies. You'd think he'd have agreed to meet with us this evening or early tomorrow. I mean, Tenet says Heinz realizes what's at stake for us on this one, and contract carriage is protected in the bill."

"Uh, yes," I answered, "and I get the feeling Heinz will support us. But let's not totally ignore the possibility of doing what I suggested last time we were here and calling in our CEO's if need be."

Dale paused a moment before saying, "Maybe you're right. I'd better alert Mr. Baker to the possibility, and you go ahead and brief Mr. Williams. Let him know we may need him to get involved, and I'll do the same."

I agreed, while adding that since we would both have other dealings with Senator Heinz, it might not pay to high-pressure the man until we heard back from Tenet. "Let's do brief our CEO's, but, as you say, let's tell them we're holding the Heinz situation in abeyance for now and that we plan on calling Tenet back if we hear nothing by next Monday."

Dale agreed.

* * *

Back in my office, I sent another update memo to PPG management, covering everything we had done to date. I resisted the urge to include our disappointment with the Heinz situation, opting instead to see if Tenet followed up in the next few days. I would alert Stan Williams with a separate memo now and get back to him next week if necessary. But I did have to report into Bob Steder, who was clearly ticked.

"Why in hell would Heinz stiff us?" Bob wondered.

I said, "Well, I'm inclined to be just a bit more charitable and assume he really was in an unexpected meeting and has a full schedule for the next day or so. And Lew Dale thinks Tenet may not be telling us about something else in the bill that worries Heinz. In any case, it's up to Tenet to follow through with us, and I'll let you know as soon as we hear from him. If that doesn't happen in the next few days, I've planned to send another heads-up to Mr. Williams. We can use him if necessary. As you'll remember, I've included him among the cc's in the status report memos, and I've heard that he and Heinz know each other well enough that they play tennis together at a club in Pittsburgh."

That was news to Steder, who said only, "Whatever works, let's do it."

I concluded by filling Bob in on Foster's call about DOE.

Steder's advice: "Don't catch a cold in the next few weeks, Ed."

CHAPTER TWENTY-FOUR

"DON'T LET THE PERFECT BE THE ENEMY OF THE GOOD"

APRIL 20, 10 A.M. -- I was on the phone with Doug Walgren. "Are you sure Sharp is having problems with the consumer protection part of the legislation?" he asked.

"That's the report from Patton Boggs," I replied.

"Well, let me talk with him and see if we can straighten him out. Then we'll see whether we need to do anything more."

"Many thanks, congressman." That was a major relief to me.

Having confirmed Doug Walgren as our point man, Dale, Ferguson, Cole and I would use the next few days to contact the other members of Sharp's subcommittee.

* * *

Washington State Democratic Rep. Al Swift knew both Foster and Tommy Boggs, who had supported his races in the past; following the visit from Foster and John Ferguson, John said Swift was now with us. I was mildly surprised at this report, since Swift was supposedly opposed to the concept of decontrolling natural gas. I could be wrong, but this seemed to be one of those times when campaign support trumped what otherwise would've been a member's opposition. Then again, the more likely reason could be that Swift would be with us on this amendment but would then vote against the bill in full committee and, if necessary, on the House floor.

Phil Pulizzi from my office and I had met with Rep. Tom Corcoran, who asked if we knew where others on the subcommittee would stand. We told him Doug Walgren was solidly in our corner and that we would let him know how things stood as our meetings progressed. That said, Corcoran did say he was leaning toward supporting us.

I had met briefly with Rep. Paul Rogers of Florida, with his energy legislative aide joining in the meeting. Rogers, whom I had met with in his role as a member of an environmental subcommittee of House Energy and Commerce, said he had been visited by George White, which didn't surprise me given LP&L's Florida connections. Rogers allowed as how White's presentation "had been persuasive" and that we could count on his vote.

On the Republican side, Reps. Jim Broyhill (NC) and Ed Madigan (IL) were solidly in our camp, gratifying to me, given PPG's good-sized presence in both of their districts. I told both men we would post a notice on the employee bulletin boards at our plants, pointing out their support for the company on this important issue.

Rep. Ralph Hall, a crusty Texan, told Cole it would be hard for him "to oppose Texaco on this one." So count Hall as a "no."

On the other hand, Jim Slattery (KS) told Rosemary O'Brien he would support us on the amendment, and Rep. Mike Oxley of Ohio told Gary Wilson of PPG and me the same thing.

So at this point, those we had seen on the Sharp subcommittee looked to be in our corner by a 7-1 margin with two undecided's and eight more members to visit. So far, Ralph Hall of Texas was the only sure Texaco supporter, while Don Ritter of Pennsylvania and Ohio's Tom Luken were undecided, and Chairman Sharp was leaning against us. Of course, Sharp was the 800-pound gorilla in the room, given that any chairperson can effectively sabotage a bill in his or her purview by stalling hearings or often just by announcing all-out opposition. I immediately briefed Mary Jo Zacchero in Walgren's office. She responded that our meeting reports were a good first step and that she would tell Walgren, and added that we still had the other 32 members of the 42-member full Energy and Commerce Committee to worry about.

"We're also waiting to hear how Mr. Walgren's meeting with Sharp goes," I offered.

"I'll let you know soon as I find out," Mary Jo said. "So how do you plan to approach Billy Tauzin? You realize that you may not need his vote in full committee."

"Well, as you know, we haven't gotten that far yet, Mary Jo. But it would be a major blow to Texaco for us to get Tauzin's support, or at least to get him not to weigh in on this one."

"He's not likely to stay silent, Ed. And don't fall into the hubris trap. Texaco will pull out all the stops to keep Billy in their camp, and you guys have other people to worry about. As folks around here are fond of saying, don't let the perfect be the enemy of the good. But if Mr. Walgren *is* able to convince Chairman Sharp to support us, it really won't matter what Tauzin does, assuming Sharp doesn't decide to sit on the bill instead of bringing it up at this time. You guys do your jobs, and we'll all worry about full committee when things get that far."

"Wouldn't Sharp be the point man on this bill in full committee as well, assuming he's talked with Chairman Dingell?" I wondered.

"I'd be surprised if not," Mary Jo replied.

"And I'm assuming that when full committee consideration is scheduled, you'll let me know the date ASAP?"

"Of course. But *I'm* assuming we're not waiting until then to start hitting all the offices."

I liked the way Zacchero was using "we" and "we're" to describe our position. "We're on the same page of the hymnal," I concluded.

CHAPTER TWENTY-FIVE

"TELL ME WHY DOE SHOULDN'T OPPOSE YOU"

APRIL 25, 9:30 A.M. -- BILL FOSTER and the First Four walked into Danny Boggs's office at the Department of Energy on Independence Avenue, S.W. We had met at the PPG offices at 8 a.m. to discuss strategy and decided to make our case as forcefully as necessary, with the goal of at least getting DOE to stay neutral on this issue. Foster had spent the previous two days brushing up on all the major provisions of the legislation, to more clearly understand Boggs's overall view in case the discussion became more wide-ranging than we anticipated.

"Okay," Boggs began while looking at Foster, "you requested this meeting. Tell me why you think DOE and the administration shouldn't oppose your position."

So immediately, Boggs was taking the offensive. Instead of asking us why DOE should support us, he was making it abundantly clear we would have to dissuade him.

Foster spent the next ten minutes carefully laying out our arguments. This time he focused on the widespread disruptions to the energy

EDWARD L. JAFFEE

market place that would result if Texaco were successful in abrogating its contracts with us. "If DOE wants to see massive dislocations in the energy markets very possibly across the board, that's what the Texaco proposal would give you. The leadership of the Senate Energy Committee, on both sides of the aisle, realized that when they decided to change the language in the bill."

"Well," Boggs replied, "there's a fair amount of hyperbole in the scenario you paint, and in any case, that's a risk we're willing to take. Look, President Reagan and Secretary Hodel really want this bill to go through, and to do so with as few changes as possible. It's our job to do everything we can to make that happen." Then he added something that surprised me, "There may already have been more changes to the legislation than we'd like to see."

Before Bill Foster or I could respond, Bob Cole joined the dialogue. "Just to be clear, our companies would also like to see the bill succeed. But there's just no way we can afford to let Texaco get away with this contract abrogation." The rest of us nodded our agreement.

"So both sides have made their positions clear," Boggs summarized.

"And we're back to where we started?" asked Foster.

"We're back to where we started. Thanks for coming in, guys. We'll let you know if matters change on our end, but if I were you, I wouldn't hold my breath on that."

* * *

In the hallway outside Boggs's office, Foster advised, "This went about as I had expected."

"Do you think McKinley and the Texaco people swayed him, assuming they got here before we did?" It was Lew Dale who asked the question.

"No," answered Foster. "I take Boggs at his word. DOE's carrying the administration's water on this one, though that was interesting, what he said about too many changes already having been made. It's just possible that with lots more fixes in the bill, the administration could signal its lukewarm support for the legislation as a whole. And that might be a major barrier to its ultimate passage. Either way, though, I'll have our people keep up the intel on where DOE stands as matters progress. It's clear that DOE's chief lobbyist, Rob Odle, has been visiting as many Energy Committee members on both sides of the Hill as he can on this bill. But I wouldn't lose much sleep about it. Chairman McClure's been their point man on the Senate bill, and he's with us, thanks in large part to Bennett Johnston. McClure's on record for us, in that virtually everybody following the legislation knows his role in revamping the bill. So he's not likely to change his stance at this point."

"True," I replied. "And it's also true that we really need to win in Phil Sharp's subcommittee."

The five of us stopped off at the DOE cafeteria for coffee and to review the picture. Foster started: "We look good in the Sharp subcommittee, assuming the chairman doesn't end up supporting Texaco."

"Have you got any specific reasons for thinking he might do that?" asked Ferguson.

"Nothing specific. But as I've said before, committee and subcommittee chairs have to look at the full bill. We just need to keep a close eye on him."

"Well, that's where we hope Walgren will do some heavy lifting for us, don't you agree?" I asked.

Foster wondered, "Is he that solidly in our camp?"

Cole answered before I could; "He looks rock solid for us." And I added, "Yes he does, but I'll touch base again this afternoon. Any reason I shouldn't let him know about the meeting we just finished?"

Foster paused for a moment, then said, "Mention it if you feel it can add anything to our leverage with him. Otherwise, I don't see what we gain by it."

"Well, I was only thinking it would be a reason for my getting back to him so soon. And he did ask Bob and me to keep him in the loop, through Mary Jo," I offered.

"Then I guess it wouldn't hurt to let him know. And re-emphasize the importance of the issue to us, and to PPG specifically."

"Right."

CHAPTER TWENTY-SIX

"HE MAY BE PLAYING US"

APRIL 26, 9:20 A.M. -- I WAS briefing Mary Jo in Walgren's office. After I reviewed the Danny Boggs meeting, I told her about Bill Foster's caveat concerning Chairman Sharp. She was surprised. "Why would he think that?"

"All he said was that committee and subcommittee chairs have to look at the big picture, the entire bill, in deciding where they stand."

"Well, obviously," Mary Jo responded. "And I'm assuming we're talking about Sharp also being concerned with aspects other than your particular fix. By now his staff should've briefed him on where the subcommittee stands on your proposed language. That's assuming you're looking to add the same language that's now in the Senate Energy version."

"That's exactly what we want," I answered.

Mary Jo continued, "The committee staffs count noses all the time, and they're usually right. You're sure about that wide margin of support you have in the subcommittee?"

"We can check again if you think it's necessary, but it looks pretty solid to us."

"Okay," Mary Jo concluded. "First I'll brief Mr. Walgren on what Foster said about Sharp's concerns with the bill. Then I'll sound out the subcommittee staff and let you know what I hear."

* * *

APRIL 26, 3:07 P.M. -- Mary Jo was on the phone with me, and the news was anything but good. "I spoke with the majority counsel on the subcommittee, Sharp's man, and he said he doesn't think Sharp will support us."

"What the hell?" I replied, louder than intended. "We had the impression he might be leaning our way."

"So you told me, Ed. But now it seems the story's different."

"Why? For Pete's sake, why?"

"I was just getting to that. Sharp thinks the consumer in Indiana won't be sufficiently protected. And before you ask, yes, he does understand the provision you guys say would protect the consumer of intrastate gas."

"Damn it," I countered, "what else does the man need to get him on our side?"

"I'm working on that now," said Mary Jo. "It could come down to a power play of sorts. Sharp has several other provisions he's concerned about in the bill. He may be playing us, using leverage to get Doug to support other stuff he wants in or out of the bill."

I felt a brief chill. So this could be a test -- an acid test -- of Walgren's support for us. Would he be willing to play ball with the subcommittee chairman in order to protect PPG's interests? Might he have to go to the mat with Sharp, a friend as well as a colleague?

I was really hoping not to remind Mary Jo of the two-way street involved between Walgren and PPG, of our thousands of employees in his Pittsburgh area district, or of the support we had given in his campaigns almost since he was first elected as a member of the "Watergate Baby" Democratic class of 1974.

Mary Jo saved me from that. "Look, Edward, we're in this thing together. Let me sit down with Doug later this afternoon and reinforce the importance of this case to you guys. Do not sic the PPG dogs on him, please. He knows the facts, and he thinks the facts are on your side. Let me do my thing and get back to you tomorrow, probably in the morning. Okay?"

"M.J.," I responded, "as Lyndon Johnson would say, 'You're a great Amurrican.' Ole Lyndon never could quite pronounce the name of the country he led, but he did get things done."

"Talk to you tomorrow, Ed."

CHAPTER TWENTY-SEVEN

"IT DOESN'T GET ANY BETTER THAN THAT"

APRIL 27, 11:05 A.M. -- TENA POKED her head into my office, saying, "Mary Jo Zacchero's on the phone. She says it's something you'll want to hear."

I had decided to wait -- with a mixture of anticipation and concern -- until Mary Jo's return call before briefing Cole, Dale, Ferguson and Foster.

"Thanks, that sounds encouraging," I replied as I grabbed the phone.

"What's the situation, MJ? Where do we stand?"

"I spoke with Doug late yesterday afternoon, Ed. He walked over to Sharp's office and the two talked for almost an hour."

"That's a long time to spend on just one issue."

"And that's just the point," Mary Jo continued. "Chairman Sharp did indeed have other concerns in the committee version of the legislation. Doug listened as Sharp went through those, one by one.

None of them covers your section of the bill, and Doug was willing to support Sharp's position on most of those items."

"What about Sharp's concern over protection of the consumer?"

"That was indeed a sticking point for Mr. Sharp. Doug showed him the language you wanted, the wording from the revised version in the Senate. Sharp and Doug eagle-eyed the wording, and Sharp said he still wasn't sure it was strong enough in protecting the consumer."

I asked, "What did Doug say then?"

It took me a moment or two to fully digest Mary Jo's answer. It was the sort of thing every Washington rep hopes for ... dreams of ... but rarely gets. "He told Sharp that on this issue, if PPG Industries has a problem, he has a problem."

"Wow!" I exclaimed. "That was one hell of a bold answer."

"Yes, but what you may not realize, Ed, is that Doug had taken an educated-guess assessment of how the full committee might vote on the overall bill, and he thinks it's gonna be a razor-thin margin either way. If Doug's right about that, Sharp needs his support when he brings the bill to full committee."

"We hadn't focused that closely on the full committee," I offered, "what with all the other balls we have in the air on this thing. Does Doug really think it could be that close a vote?"

"I haven't had a chance to parse his discussion with Sharp that closely. But I doubt that Doug would try to bluff his subcommittee chairman. So, don't you want to know what Mr. Sharp said?"

"You bet I do."

"Sharp told Doug, in words something like these, 'Well, you've seen my side on most of these other parts of the bill, so I guess I can give way and agree with you on this one, if it really means that much to you.'"

"MJ," I answered, "tell Doug we greatly appreciate his active support, and it should go without saying that we're tremendously grateful for all you've done as well."

"No problem, Ed. And not so incidentally, Doug's ready to push for your language in the subcommittee markup, which looks like it may take place in the next two or three weeks. Sharp may be willing to put your wording into the version the members will see at markup. It would be the same language that's in the revised version of the Senate bill."

"It doesn't get any better than that," I said. "Thanks again, M J."

* * *

I got back to the office and immediately called Bob Steder and then sent an update to PPG management, emphasizing Walgren's active support for us. Next, I asked Tena to contact the rest of the First Four and Bill Foster. We agreed to meet at 4 p.m. in Lew Dale's offices at Air Products.

CHAPTER TWENTY-EIGHT

"THE CHAIRMAN MAY WANT HIS WORDING"

APRIL 28, 4 P.M. -- IN MY euphoria over Doug Walgren's having gone to bat for us with Chairman Sharp, I'd ignored one possible dark cloud. It was Bob Cole who pointed out that, "Let's not be so sure we want the same exact wording at this stage in the House as we have in Senate Energy. There's a lot of turf jealousy between the two houses of Congress, and a chairman, particularly a strong one like John Dingell, may well want to see *his* committee's wording go forward in conference committee. And that's assuming we can get our position accepted in full committee."

"That's a fair point," I conceded. "Should I raise it with Mary Jo?"

"Not just yet," said Dale. "Why not let it rest for a few days, until we find out when Sharp is scheduling his subcommittee markup? There'll still be plenty of time to try to bring about a change, if that's really what we want to do."

"On that matter," offered Ferguson, "it seems to me it's a question of the point Bob just made versus the advantage of having the same language in the bills in both houses of Congress, and avoiding the need for that provision to be noodled over in conference committee." *(A conference committee is a group of legislators from both sides of the Hill -- Senate and House -- appointed to try to iron out differences between the versions of legislation passed by each body. If they agree on the wording, a conference report is written, to accompany the merged bill as it goes back to the Senate and House floor for final approval and then on to the president's desk. Absent that approval, the bill may either be referred back to one or both houses for reconsideration, or it may die.)*

"True," said Cole. "But we all know how Chairman Dingell operates, and I really think we're risking his disapproval of our position if we push the issue before he takes his shot at the wording. In any event, I do agree we can wait until Sharp schedules the subcommittee markup."

Foster spoke up. "I think Bob has the right idea here. And we have time to think about it, at any rate, and when the time is right, I can ask our Bill O'Hara to sound out Dingell. For now, let's just build off of Walgren's support and go from there."

We turned our attention to the bigger picture. As Cole put it, "If Walgren is right, we have a battle on our hands in the full House Energy and Commerce Committee. And that means that in addition to our emphasis on Senate Energy, we now have to worry, sooner than we thought, about the 42 members of Chairman Dingell's full committee in the House."

That thought was sobering enough, and then Foster added, "Plus, we now know that DOE may continue to go full-bore despite what looks like many battles on various parts of the bill. Let's not forget that this issue is still a key piece of President Reagan's agenda, unless they see too many changes for their liking."

"It still fits the old saying about anything worth winning being worth fighting for," added Cole.

CHAPTER TWENTY-NINE

"LEAVING THE FIGHT TO TEXACO"

APRIL 29, 9 A.M. -- THINKING DOWNSTREAM, I was reviewing the roster of the full House Energy and Commerce Committee. In terms of relationships with our companies, it looked as if the pickings were pretty slim. Democrats who I knew had no direct links to plants or labs of our four companies included Dick Ottinger (NY), Henry Waxman (CA), Cardiss Collins (IL), Jim Florio and Matt Rinaldo (both NJ), Wayne Dowdy (MS), Mickey Leland (TX) and Bill Richardson (NM).

On the Republican side, I knew the First Four had no corporate links to Bob Whittaker (KS), Jack Fields (TX), Carlos Moorhead, Jim Bates and Bill Dannemeyer (all CA), Norm Lent (NY), Tom Bliley (VA), Howard Nielsen (UT) and Tom Tauke (IA).

That totaled 17 of the 42 members on the full committee, and while a few of those would be visited by companies in the Second Six, it was clear that our group would have to make a major effort in what might be a brief amount of time.

It seemed logical that at least Synar, Fields, Hall and Leland, from "Oil Patch" states, would side with Texaco. I made a note to sound out the other companies in our coalition on the subject, knowing that Texaco had an advantage over us in numbers if not in depth: they would undoubtedly urge their nationwide network of gasoline station owners -- whether independently operated or owned by Texaco -- to write letters or make calls supporting their position, to their House and Senate members. And they might well ask their stockholders to make calls or send letters as well. Those letters or calls might help somewhat, but I figured they were no substitute for face-to-face contacts.

* * *

MAY 22, 9:20 A.M. -- My mental gymnastics were interrupted by a phone call from Ralph Zaaenga of Phillips Petroleum, with welcome news. True to his word, Ralph had, while seeming casual about it, drilled into the depths of the American Petroleum Institute's concerns about our issue.

"So Ed," he reported, "I checked with a couple of higher-ups at API, and as best I can tell, supporting Texaco on this one is not on their plate. They're following the overall legislation pretty closely, given that several major oil companies also deal in natural gas, but they're leaving this fight to Texaco. And I'm assuming that's good news for you, right?"

I didn't want to seem overeager in responding, and said only, "Well, it simplifies matters, so I'm glad to get the report. Thanks for doing this, Ralph. And by the way, I did check, and Sharon would love to take in another concert with you and Elspeth. How about if I ask her to call Elspeth, and our wives can set it up?"

"Sounds like a plan," came the reply. "Glad I could help."

No sooner had I hung up the phone than Tena buzzed, saying that Lew Dale was on line two.

"Got some interesting news, Edward," he began. I contacted our company chairman, Dexter Baker, after our last session with Tenet. Baker talked directly with Heinz."

"You're ahead of me in following up," I allowed, thinking that Dale had jumped the gun on our agreement to wait for further word from the Heinz office before briefing our CEO's. "So what's the story? What did Heinz say?"

"Mr. Baker said Heinz made no commitment, but basically he got the impression that Heinz sees our point on this issue, and he did say he opposes contract abrogation."

"Sounds as if Tenet did indeed talk with his boss, then."

"Well, I can't say that for sure. Heinz did tell Mr. Baker what we had already heard, that he doesn't like the way McClure and Johnston are crafting the overall compromise proposal. I was so concerned at that mixed message that I didn't ask Mr. Baker for a clarification."

"Well, the key point still seems to be that Heinz told your chairman he may support our position, if I understand you correctly. I would think that means we list him as 'leaning for' us on the vote, wouldn't you?"

"As far as I know, he didn't *firmly* commit, but that's sure as hell what I'm hoping it means, Ed."

"Okay, I'll let Bill Foster and the others know. Thanks for the report, Lew."

I first called Bob Steder with the news; he was as uncertain but hopeful as Lew and I were. "So we still don't really know for sure how our home state senior senator will vote on this one, right?"

"That's true," I admitted.

CHAPTER THIRTY

COUNTING NOSES

MAY 3, 9:12 A.M. -- ROSEMARY O'BRIEN was on the phone with a heads-up. "If you haven't already seen today's *Wall Street Journal*, take a look at the lead editorial. It seems the media relations people for our friends from Texaco have been more than a little busy."

"Why?" I asked. "What'd it say?"

"I could give you a recap or send a fax, but I think you'd rather see it for yourself."

"No problem; there's a shop in our lobby that carries the papers. I'll check it out now. And thanks for the alert, Rosemary."

The editorial, basically a plea for natural gas decontrol legislation to pass, was headlined "Wasted Energy," and it seemed obvious Texaco had spoken at some length with the editorial page staff of *The Journal*. The salient paragraph for us was this:

"A group of senators led by Sen. Bennett Johnston (D.-La.) has included an exception in the gas decontrol bill for direct sale purchases, generally made by large industrial users ... in places like Louisiana, Texas and Oklahoma. These intrastate sales would remain below market prices while controls on interstate sales would be loosened or eliminated."

The editorial went on to claim that the senators backing this move have "no apparent regard for market economics."

I phoned Bill Foster immediately and sent him a copy of the editorial, then did the same for Bob Steder, adding that while Texaco's timing was good -- with the vote in Senate Energy and Natural Resources set to take place tomorrow -- it seemed that going to the business paper of record was an indication they felt they were losing the fight in that committee.

Foster called back before I could have Tena call the rest of the First Four to see if they had seen the editorial. Bill's comment essentially mirrored mine to Steder, but he said he would check with Senator Johnston to make sure we were still solid with him, McClure and Ford.

Meanwhile, given the length of the bill, the markup and committee vote in Senate Energy, to begin tomorrow, might well take two days, and both Bob Cole and Rosemary O'Brien had just called with the same suggestion: we needed a meeting of the combined coalitions -- the First Four and Second Six -- to go over our final readings of the members of the committee. We decided to hold it in the PPG offices at 11 that morning.

* * *

MAY 3, 11 A.M. -- The meeting went fairly quickly. By now, everyone had seen the editorial. Foster had done his double-checking, and there seemed to be no change in backing for our language to stay in the bill.

With that, and since markup was to begin tomorrow, everyone needed to make final contacts with their assigned members of the Senate Energy Committee. We focused on the members of the 22-member committee with whom we had made visits. As for the others, we had sent our briefing papers to their staff and followed with phone calls to make sure they received them.

On balance, the final pre-markup review left us off balance, beginning with the conservative assumption that, of the seven committee members with whom we had no ties and would therefore list as "undecided," we would get the votes of two of them: Cochran of Mississippi, thanks to Bill Simpson, and either Melcher of Montana or Wallop of Wyoming. By our calculations, that meant we might not have support from Matsunaga of Hawaii, Weicker of Connecticut, Levin of Michigan, Domenici of New Mexico and either Melcher or Wallop. We were down by at least 5-0, in support for the McClure-Johnston-Ford compromise legislation.

We then added Senators Bentsen and Nickles, from Texas and Oklahoma respectively, to those expected to vote "No" on the proposal. So, at least seven to none against us.

On the other side of the ledger, we figured Senators Ford (who had helped draft the revised bill with McClure and Johnston), Heinz, Johnston, McClure, Hatfield, Bumpers and presumably Metzenbaum, based on Jim Wilderotter's earlier comments, were with us, with "Scoop" Jackson's vote in limbo until his return. That would leave us tied at seven votes for and seven against.

The major imponderable, and thus our biggest concern going into the markup, was how the rest of the committee members would vote. They included Nunn (despite our pull-out-all-the-stops efforts), Bradley, Murkowski, Wallop or Melcher, Warner, and, for purposes of the count, Jackson.

Murkowski, from Alaska, had told Bill Foster he was juggling inputs from several companies on a variety of sections of the legislation and hadn't yet decided how he would vote. Tommy Boggs was expected to call the senator, but hadn't yet reached him.

So, as I and others had figured all along, this one was simply too close to call. Foster said he would check to see if Bennett Johnston had contacted Senator Long, and if not, Bill would suggest that this might be a good time for Johnston to make the call to Long. Again, given Long's power base in the Senate as ranking member of the Finance Committee, it could be a major help if he were willing to make a friendly call to one or more of the undecideds.

But we had no reason to believe Long would or would not agree to make those calls. All in all, it seemed we might just have a restless night's sleep going into this major committee markup and vote.

CHAPTER THIRTY-ONE

"A TIE'S AS GOOD AS A WIN"

MAY 4, 9:10 A.M. -- COLE, DALE, Ferguson, Foster and I were gathered in the packed hall outside the Senate Energy and Natural Resources Committee room; the session was scheduled to begin at 9:30. Members of the Second Six were there as well, in clusters talking with their outside attorneys.

Foster reported that he had spoken last night with Bennett Johnston, who had said he would call Senator Long, but added that he didn't think it would make much difference at this point. Bill added that Johnston seemed "calm and composed."

The same could not be said of me or the others in the First Four. We were clearly nervous, and not alone in that. Cole spotted Texaco's Don Annett across the hall, huddled with attorney John Camp. Camp seemed placid, and while it was impossible for me to read anything from Annett's face, he seemed fidgety to me.

The committee room doors opened at 9:15 and everybody poured in. The First Four and Bill Foster quickly took seats in a back row. The room was filled when Chairman McClure gaveled the session to order. Bob Cole noted the absence of Senator Jackson, adding that

"It looks like there won't be any tie votes, with only 21 members here."

As the ranking minority member of the committee, Senator Johnston sat next to McClure.

For the next three hours, the committee plodded through the bill, section by section, with a member of the staff beginning to read each section aloud, getting through the first sentence, and then being interrupted by a request that the section "be considered as read and open for amendment."

By 12:30, when the committee recessed for lunch, it was apparent that, at the pace they were going, they would not get to our section until tomorrow, assuming they stayed until 5 p.m. We decided to meet in the cafeteria. Foster phoned Patton Boggs and asked that a paralegal be sent to sit in at the markup and to come and get us if the committee got as far as section 291. Bill figured that with 25 sections to be considered before they would get to Section 316, we would have more than ample time to come back into the markup session. And in any event, we would all return tomorrow morning if necessary.

Then Foster went to Bennett Johnston's office and spoke with Johnston's legislative aide for energy issues, Betsy Moeller, who told him that it likely would indeed be tomorrow before our section would be considered. Moeller had no new information to offer about our chances to prevail on Section 316, or what she called the "for resale" language.

Our group decided to hang around in the cafeteria for much of the afternoon, just to be sure we wouldn't be caught off guard by an accelerated markup. Each of us did his best to appear calm and cool; I only knew that whenever I focused on the upcoming committee vote, I felt restless and eager to get at the meat of the matter.

A little after 5 p.m., the Patton Boggs paralegal came into the cafeteria and told us the markup was at Section 271 of the bill, and that McClure and Johnston had just announced their plan to adjourn for the day at about 5:45 p.m. and resume promptly at 9 a.m. tomorrow.

Cole, Dale, Ferguson and I, plus Foster, went to Bob's office at Kaiser. I phoned Steder and left a brief status report, and the other three Washington reps contacted their principals as well. Foster made a final check on the status of Senator Nunn and reported that the senator was still uncertain but now supposedly leaning toward our position, and we then made a last review of where we thought every committee member would be on the issue tomorrow: no changes; still basically a tie vote.

I was musing that a tie would be a win for us, since Texaco needed a majority to overturn the McClure-Johnston-Ford amendment to Section 316 of the bill.

Tomorrow would be crucial for all of us.

CHAPTER THIRTY-TWO

"WHAT THE HELL HAPPENED?"

MAY 5, 8:30 A.M. -- THE CROWD in the hall outside the committee room was smaller this morning; obviously, the committee had addressed the concerns of many in yesterday's long session.

The doors opened promptly at 8:45 a.m. and the five of us, Bill Foster included, again took seats in a back row. Chairman McClure gaveled the supposed 9 a.m. session to order at 9:22, just as we were beginning to wonder if some backroom deals being finalized might be delaying this morning's markup.

I noticed some empty seats on the dais and made a quick count. There were eighteen senators in attendance. Jackson was still absent, and three other members were evidently satisfied that their particular area(s) of concern had been addressed yesterday, or maybe they had urgent constituent business. In all likelihood, they would return for the final committee vote on the bill.

The members moved slowly through the various sections of the legislation. When they reached Section 315, just ahead of our issue, I noticed that Cole, Dale and Ferguson were leaning forward. Foster sat calmly upright in his seat.

Finally, at 11:05, the clerk began reading Section 316, including our "not for resale" language as crafted by Chairman McClure and Senators Bentsen and Ford. There were still eighteen committee members on hand.

The chairman asked that the section be considered as read and that it be open for amendment. Immediately, Senator Lloyd Bentsen spoke up, saying he had "an amendment at the desk," requesting that it be read by the clerk. Normally, amendments are lengthy enough that the sponsor requests that it be considered as read and that "I be allowed five minutes to explain the amendment."

This time, however, the proposed amendment was brief, to the point, and all too recognizable to the First Four and Foster. It was almost but not entirely the exact wording that was in the original version of S. 615: "Any two parties to a first-sale, direct sale, not-for-resale contract for natural gas will have until January 1, 1985, to renegotiate said contract to their mutual agreement. In the instance of failure to reach such an accord, either party may market out." Bentsen had then added a few extraneous words, apparently so that McClure would not ask him to simply vote against the existing Section 316 instead of introducing an amendment to delete it.

I whispered to Foster, seated to my right, that "Texaco management, their attorneys, John Camp and Annett must figure they have the votes. Otherwise, wouldn't they have asked for one slice less than the full loaf on this?"

"Maybe, and maybe not. I still think we're gonna win this thing, probably by a razor-thin margin."

* * *

It was logical for Bentsen, a Texan, to be carrying Texaco's water on the amendment. He used his five minutes to restate every argument Texaco had been making from the start, focusing mainly on the "blatant unfairness" of the committee staff draft to "the vast majority of companies in Louisiana, Texas and some other states" and the "sweetheart sort of deal a select few companies" in Louisiana were getting. And he tried to turn one of our own arguments on its head, saying that if the original language in the bill were not reinstated as in his amendment, it could lead to major disruptions in the natural gas marketplace.

I looked at Cole, who was shaking his head in amazement. Foster whispered that some Bentsen staffer or committee minority staffer "really missed the point" on that argument.

Senator Johnston spoke up against the amendment, reflecting our thoughts on Bentsen's last point, and, as expected, emphasizing the sanctity of contract argument.

No one else spoke on the amendment, and at 11:13 it was time to vote. Chairman McClure asked for the yeas and nays, and the voice vote was obviously too close to call. Senator Bentsen requested a recorded vote. I noticed that at least a few members of the committee seemed uncomfortable at having to record their vote on a contentious issue.

The next eleven minutes were increasingly surprising to me, as almost every member voted the way we had anticipated, something uncommon in a committee of this size. As the committee clerk continued through the roll call, Foster offered a slight smile; he and the ten companies in our merged coalition seemed to have almost nailed the vote count. Lew Dale whispered to me, "I wonder if we could hire ourselves out as whips." *(One job of the majority and minority whip and their assistants in each body of Congress is to get an accurate advance count of how a vote is likely to turn out on the floor.)*

The vote went like this:

For the Texaco amendment: Senators Bentsen, Matsunaga, Melcher, Murkowski, Levin, Warner, Wallop and Weicker. That was eight members, with one yet to come.

Against the Texaco amendment, and thus for our position: Senators McClure, Johnston, Ford, Metzenbaum, Cochran, Domenici, Bumpers, and to our great relief, Nunn. And again, that totaled eight, with one still to vote.

Then came the two stunners: Senator Heinz voted *for* the Texaco amendment! We were down, 9-8.

But then, Senator Nickles of Oklahoma voted *against* it. A 9-9 tie!

I figured that each of the First Four had essentially the same two thoughts: "Thank God for the tie vote," giving us the win over Texaco in committee. And, "What the hell just happened with Heinz and Nickles?"

We were all somewhat shaken, and quickly decided to go outside to chew it over. I spoke first, "Well, I'm stumped. We just won the vote, but Heinz deserted us. And why on earth would Don Nickles desert Texaco?"

"I don't know," replied Foster. "And we'll see if we can find out about Nickles, Ed. Meanwhile, you and Lew just might want to check on brother Heinz."

"You get the understatement award of the day," offered Dale.

"So what's our next step?" asked Ferguson, as Bob Cole nodded his agreement with the question.

"Well," I ventured, "let's go back to my office and figure that out. Bill, you coming?"

"I need to get back to my shop to brief Tommy and at least look at some other work that's been piling up," answered Foster.

Had we stayed through the conclusion of the day's markup, we would have witnessed countless arguments and counter-arguments over a myriad of issues in the bill. Finally, at 6:30 p.m., McClure had unveiled a surprise. Noting that there were still provisions in the measure to consider, he had adjourned the markup, stating that it would resume "at the call of the chair." When cornered by reporters in the hall, he had said he had no idea when that would be.

So while we were protected in our part of the bill, by the narrowest of margins, we had no clue when, or even if, the Senate Energy Committee would report the measure to the floor. And of course, in theory, Texaco might still be able to work some mischief into the bill, either by convincing one of their supporters to offer some sort of an amendment giving them relief or by trying to have committee report language inserted that would vitiate our victory in some way.

CHAPTER THIRTY-THREE

"A COUPLE OF LINES..."

MAY 5, 11:55 A.M. -- THE FIRST Four were in a cab heading back to the PPG Washington office. While all four of us were greatly relieved at the tie vote and our win, we were still mystified by Senator Heinz's vote.

"I mean, I know he had problems with the way various compromise deals were made among committee members," I mused. "But to vote against two major companies from his own state (PPG and Air Products) and in favor of a Texas company just doesn't seem to make sense."

"Yeah, and I expect I'll be getting a call from Dexter Baker," Dale muttered while showing his disappointment.

I shook my head and added, "I just don't get it."

"Hold on," said Ferguson. "I just remembered something. My brother-in-law is the business columnist for the Pittsburgh Press."

Dale and I looked at each other and both said pretty much the same thing at the same time: "Driver, forget about 1730 Rhode

DODGING THE BULLET

Island Avenue; take us to 1875 I Street instead." That was home to Georgia-Pacific's Washington office.

We got to John's office and sat at the conference table while he spent fifteen minutes on the phone with his brother-in-law, explaining the situation and the Heinz vote. When John hung up, Cole asked, "So what's the deal? Did he say he'd write something up?"

"He said he'd check with the business editor and see. I suspect that most likely, he'll have a couple of lines in his Sunday column."

That was about what I figured would happen, and we adjourned, with plans to meet at 3 p.m. at PPG, with Foster attending and reporting on what, if anything, he had learned about the Nickles vote. One thing was for sure: Texaco would be all over Nickles on this one.

* * *

I got back to my office just before 1 p.m., having grabbed a sandwich after leaving Ferguson's office, and immediately fired off a memo to the PPG management team I'd updated earlier.

Next on the "to do" list was a call to Bob Steder.

"I've been wondering when you'd call, Ed. How'd we do?"

"It's the classic 'good news, bad news' story. Bottom line, we did great, with one major caveat, Bob. There were eighteen members of the committee there, and we won on a 9-9 tie vote."

"Excellent! So what's the caveat?"

"Heinz voted the wrong way."

"Damn," came the reply. "I guess I never felt certain of his vote, but still …"

"I know, and I just sent a memo to you and the management team."

There was silence on the other end, so I continued by briefing Steder on the call Ferguson had just made to his brother-in-law.

Steder laughed and said, "Then, I'll be checking the papers. So what's next for you and the other guys?"

"We have a 3 p.m. meeting here to dope out what we do next. I'll keep you in the loop."

CHAPTER THIRTY-FOUR

"ONCE YOU'VE WON, STOP"

MAY 5, 3:05 P.M. -- TENA JOINED us in a celebratory toast with soft drinks, and the First Four settled in to hear Bill Foster's report.

Except, there was nothing to report. "Senator Nickles and his staff are being extremely tight-lipped on this one," Foster began. "We've gotten nothing yet, but our people are on it. Anyway, we can bet Texaco is on his case, big-time, and we'll probably have a hard time keeping him with us when the bill reaches the Senate floor. And by the way, the bill is still in committee. They didn't finish it, and McClure adjourned the markup subject to his call to resume. He said later he has no idea when that will happen."

"I'm surprised," I said.

"Don't be," answered Bill. "There are loads of contentious issues in this baby, and we'll still need to be alert to whatever tricks Texaco may have up their sleeve."

I shook my head in resignation, and turned to Ferguson, asking if he cared to add anything about "the other surprise this morning." John gave an abbreviated account of the phone call he'd made.

"You guys sure that's what you want to do?" wondered Foster. "I mean, Heinz is a home state senator to your two companies. You're going to need him on other votes in the future. And there's also that key rule in lobbying: 'Once you've won, stop.'"

That was a "hmmm" moment for me. Maybe I should have thought about the possible consequences instead of getting caught up in the heat of the moment. "You may have a point, Bill," I offered. "And we really were never able to positively nail down his vote in advance, despite what he told Lew's chairman, Dexter Baker."

"Well, it's just a thought," said Foster. "So shouldn't we turn our attention to Phil Sharp's House subcommittee?"

Before anyone could answer, Tena came in and told me Mary Jo Zacchero was on the line. I excused myself, went into the next room and took the call.

"Congratulations," Mary Jo began. "That was apparently a squeaker, but you guys won. Now, the congressman and I have an idea. Texaco is licking its wounds right now, and I suspect Sharp's Subcommittee on Fossil and Synthetic Fuels is not on their front burner today."

"Valid point, M.J."

"Okay, so I spoke with Doug an hour ago, and we both thought this might be the time to catch Texaco off guard by opening the markup and bringing your provision up for a vote in subcommittee tomorrow. Doug just got off the line with Chairman Sharp, who's willing to do that if Doug really wants him to."

I was thinking that Walgren had more sway with the subcommittee chairman than I'd realized, until I recalled Mary Jo's earlier comment about Doug's reading of a razor-thin vote margin in full committee. Apparently Sharp had the same thing in mind.

"That's a hell of an idea," I responded, "and you're certain that Sharp is willing to raise our issue at this point?"

"That's what we suggested, actually it was a request, and Sharp agreed to go ahead if Doug wants to."

"Can you hold the phone for a minute? I've got the other three guys and Bill Foster here, and I'd expect we'll have to line up most of the eighteen votes on the subcommittee between now and tomorrow morning, right?"

"Probably so," came the reply. "But I was gonna discuss tactics with you before you start on that job. I'll hold while you check."

I went back to the conference room and began with, "Well, this is interesting. Mary Jo Zacchero, Walgren's energy L.A. (*legislative assistant*) is holding for me. She says that with Texaco obviously focused on today's Senate committee vote, she and Walgren felt tomorrow would be the perfect time for a Sharp subcommittee vote on the staff draft, with Doug offering our fix to that section of the bill. Doug's gotten agreement from Sharp to do it that way, if we'd like."

"Wait a second, Ed," countered Bob Cole. "Won't there be members of the subcommittee who would object to moving that fast on the bill? I mean, as we all know, our issue is just one of dozens if not hundreds under consideration. And then too, isn't it really unusual to begin a markup with a section late in the bill?"

"That may be true," I responded. "But both Doug and Sharp realize the full committee vote will be extremely tight, just as we saw in Senate Energy this morning, and Sharp and apparently full committee chairman Dingell as well, must really need Walgren's vote. Besides that, I'm pretty sure a subcommittee chairman can handle a markup pretty much as he wants to, assuming he lets his members know in advance and can convince them not to object. There'd be tradeoffs involved, for sure."

"Ah, to be a swing vote now that spring is here," said Foster. "Do we think we can round up a majority of the eighteen votes we'll need between now and markup tomorrow?"

"Mary Jo just told me she's ready to suggest specific tactics for us."

Cole answered, "We'll be blitzed getting this done between now and tomorrow. But I'm game if the rest of you are." Ferguson and

Dale both nodded, and Foster added, "Then let's do it. Can you put Mary Jo on the speaker phone?"

I went back to the phone, apologized for the delay and filled Zacchero in on our decision, then said, "I'm putting you on the horn so we can all take part. We're interested. So, what's your plan?"

"Okay," she began. "Here's our thinking: Roughly speaking, we can divide the subcommittee into four loose blocs: liberal Democrats, moderate-to-conservative Democrats, moderate-to-conservative Republicans and conservative Republicans. Doug's a moderate Democrat, so he's in the second bloc. Now, it's possible that the four key members can do most of the heavy lifting for you by lining up support from others in their blocs. But just in case, let me give you my reading on the other seventeen members. Take notes, and you can decide who sees whom, with the understanding that Doug will provide as much help as he can, on our side of the aisle."

I looked over at Foster, who smiled and said, "Don't think we can do any better than that. Let's go for it."

Mary Jo began. "Liberal Democrats are Paul Rogers, Tim Wirth, Ed Markey and Al Gore." We were writing fast. "Moderate-to-conservative Dems include Chairman Sharp, and Doug will make sure he's with us on the vote, plus Al Swift, Tom Luken, Wayne Dowdy, Mickey Leland, Mike Synar and of course, Doug himself. Got that so far?"

"Dowdy is generally conservative, though he has taken a few moderate stances this year," I said. "And at any rate, I think we'll ask Bill Simpson of Thivenot and Simpson, one of the six other folks we're affiliated with in this battle, to see Dowdy. Simpson's really tight with the entire Mississippi delegation."

"Good," replied Zacchero. "Now, everybody with me so far?"

I looked around, and everyone nodded. "Yup," I answered.

"Okay, so the moderate-to-conservative Republicans include Tom Corcoran, Jim Slattery and Don Ritter, and the conservative Republicans are Ralph Hall from Texas, Jim Broyhill, Ed Madigan and

Mike Oxley. Our suggestion is that the four of you, plus Mr. Foster and anyone else you can line up in the next hour or so, visit as many of those offices as you can between now and tomorrow. Obviously, you're not gonna waste much time with the two Texans, Hall and Leland, or with Synar from Oklahoma, although I understand Senator Nickles did support you in Senate Energy this morning."

Bob Cole spoke up, identifying himself and asking, "Will chairman Sharp send out the markup notice within the next hour?"

"Likely so, Bob, or at least within two hours."

"Okay," Cole continued. "Then there should be no surprises when we hit all these offices. I mean, they should all know what's on schedule for tomorrow."

"That's true."

"Then, is it a go with us?" I asked. Everyone agreed, and Foster concluded, "Let's get cracking."

To Mary Jo, I added, "It seems I'm always thanking you, M. J. And I'll have all of us keep you posted every few hours, if you'll be in the office."

"No problem, Ed. And I expect to be here until ten tonight or so."

After I hung up, Bob Cole raised another question. "What about the Second Six? I mean, other than Bill Simpson? We at least owe them a heads-up as to what we're doing."

"Absolutely," I agreed. "Let me call O'Brien and King soon as we're done here. I suspect they'll be more than happy to let us do our thing on this, and to offer whatever help they can. And I need to track down Simpson anyway."

CHAPTER THIRTY-FIVE

"EIGHTEEN HOURS TO COMPLETE OUR BLITZKRIEG"

MAY 5, 3:50 P.M. --THOSE EARLIER thoughts I'd had about being in a war on several fronts were foremost in my mind as we got about the job of once again divvying up our assignments.

Cole began our "who sees whom" meeting by seconding Zacchero's suggestion that we skip not only Ralph Hall and Leland of Texas, but also Mike Synar of Oklahoma. "It'd be a long shot for us to land any of those guys, and any one of them might just alert Texaco to what's happening tomorrow. And that's assuming they won't have already told Annett."

I said, "Right," as Foster and the others said variants of "good point." Then we turned to our assignments.

"Rather than having each of us take one of the four blocs," I suggested, "we each have fairly-strong-to-strong ties to various members of the subcommittee, and we've seen many of them already. How about if we speak up for our druthers first, and then follow the Walgren-Zacchero idea for the rest of them?"

"That might work," said Dale. "Do you see a need to let Zacchero know first?"

"I don't think she really cares how we do it, just so long as we hit all the offices we need to," I said.

"Okay. It's your idea, so why don't you go first?" replied Dale.

"Well," I began, focusing first on the members who had already indicated their support on the issue, "PPG's pretty tight with both Madigan and Broyhill, and I think Rosemary O'Brien will want to join me in visiting Madigan's office if she's available." Ed Madigan's district was square in the middle of Illinois farming country, where CF Industries was big.

I added, "And my immediate boss, Gary Wilson, is close to Mike Oxley from their college days in Ohio, so if nobody objects, I'll take him as well."

"Do it," answered Cole and Foster simultaneously.

Ferguson noted, "That's all of the conservative Republicans except Hall."

"Anyone else you're particularly close to, Ed?" asked Foster.

"Well, I saw Paul Rogers, from Florida, earlier, after George White had already pretty much convinced him to support us. And I've worked on and off with his staff on environmental issues. So I'll stop by just to be sure they're on board for tomorrow's vote."

"Then you've got those four, plus Walgren, of course," said Foster.

Cole spoke up, saying he'd be more comfortable with the Zacchero plan, and that he would take the moderate-to-conservative Republicans: Corcoran, Slattery and Ritter, and added that when we got to full committee, he would work on Chairman Dingell, presumably joining Patton Boggs' Bill O'Hara, the former Michigan congressman.

Dale beat Ferguson to the punch, saying, "I'll take a shot at the moderate-to-conservative Democrats. That'd be Swift and Luken, and we're leaving Leland and Synar out as lost causes. Of course, we're assuming Sharp will be with us, per Walgren, right?"

"Right," I answered.

John Ferguson was both smiling and shaking his head as he said, "Thanks a bunch, guys. You're leaving me with the liberal Democrats, Wirth, Markey and Gore. That's assuming Jaffee gets Paul Rogers."

"Piece of cake for you," I rejoined. "Just focus on Chairman Sharp's support for the amendment."

"You sure *you* don't wanna take these guys, Ed?"

"You'll do fine, John. And check our earlier discussions on which of the Second Six folks to contact for support, if you really think you'll need it." John gave a dismissive wave and said, "I'll manage. So do we meet someplace late tonight to compare notes, and if so, where?"

"How about 10:15 in the South Capitol Street lobby of the Rayburn House Office Building?" I asked, adding, "That'll give me time to check in with Mary Jo just before 10."

At that moment, Tena came in and said Zacchero had just left a message that markup was set for 10 a.m. tomorrow in the subcommittee hearing room on the second floor of Rayburn.

"That leaves us eighteen hours to complete our little blitzkrieg," said Foster. "So what are we doing cooling our heels here? Let's get moving."

CHAPTER THIRTY-SIX

"WHERE IS RALPH HALL ...?"

MAY 5, 6:07 P.M. – AFTER BRIEFING O'Brien and King, I decided to take the low-hanging fruit first and see Reps. Broyhill and Madigan. I had first gotten Bill Simpson out of a meeting at his law offices, explained the situation and asked if he could try to lock up Wayne Dowdy. "Of co-ess," came the drawl. "Ah'll do that soon as meetin' is ovuh."

I thanked him and quickly set about phoning my assigned members' offices, mentioning that the subcommittee markup would be tomorrow morning and gaining agreement from them to meet briefly with me by 8:30 this evening. It was not unusual for Hill staffers to work late hours in the height of a congressional session, and today was no different.

Rep. Broyhill had agreed to see me personally, and Rosemary O'Brien said she would join me at 6:45 to see Rep. Madigan.

Jim Broyhill was a soft-spoken Southern gentleman with a large PPG Industries fiber glass production plant in his district. We had talked several times on issues of concern to the company, and he had generally been in our corner.

EDWARD L. JAFFEE

This time, after I explained the situation, he had two questions: first, "Where is Ralph Hall on this issue? You know he's ranking minority on the full committee."

I had to be candid. "Well, congressman, as you know, Texaco is a major factor in his state. I fully expect him to support them by opposing our language in the staff draft."

"And again, how important is this issue to PPG?"

"If Texaco wins on this one, it honestly could put us out of business in Louisiana, costing over two thousand jobs."

"That's Louisiana, not North Carolina, but it's still a lot of jobs, and if it really means that much to you guys, I'll support you."

Broyhill had just balanced what might be pressure from the ranking member of the full committee versus the importance of this issue to a major employer in his own district, and had decided in favor of PPG. I replied, "Thank you, congressman, and I'll be sure to let our plant manager in your district know that you're with us on a key issue."

* * *

MAY 5, 6:43 P.M. -- Rosemary met me just outside of Ed Madigan's offices. As we walked into the suite, I pointed to a decorative quilt hanging among a slew of photos on one of the walls. "That was made by employees at our Mt. Zion, Illinois, glass plant and presented to Madigan seven years ago by our plant manager at the time."

"Sounds like you guys are in like Flynn with the congressman."

"Probably no more so than CF Industries is, especially given his interest in agriculture, wouldn't you say?"

"I agree," said Rosemary.

The appointments secretary motioned us into the congressman's office. Madigan was a tall man with dark wavy hair just turning a bit grey, and a solid build. He shook my hand, said, "Hello, Ed," and gave Rosemary a brief hug. This meeting would not be a challenge.

I quickly outlined the situation. Madigan had not yet been briefed by his L.A. about the markup tomorrow, and wondered aloud, "Why the accelerated action by Sharp?"

I shot a quick glance at Rosemary, with a barely perceptible shake of my head. She said nothing, so I explained. "We had a squeaker of a win on this issue this morning in Senate Energy. Texaco had to get our language out of the bill, and lost on a tie vote. We've been working with Doug Walgren over on this side of the Hill, what with our having nine plants and labs in his district in and around Pittsburgh, and he got Sharp to agree to move on this one tomorrow."

"Why?" asked Madigan.

I answered, "First, both Walgren and Sharp see the full committee vote on the bill as too close to call, and Sharp really wants Walgren's support on it. And second, our thinking is that Texaco will still be focused on looking for ways to revisit the Senate vote they just lost, and not on a quick House subcommittee vote."

"And you guys want to strike while the iron is hot? That sort of thing?"

"That's pretty much it," I answered.

"Rosemary, you agree with this?"

"Absolutely, congressman."

"Then okay, I'm with you." Madigan paused a moment, then added, "Maybe we can work this out as a voice vote. I'll check with Sharp's office and see what they think."

Madigan's thinking made sense, given that on any vote not of particular importance to them but on a possibly controversial issue, many members of Congress prefer not to have their vote recorded. Those votes often are used, and just as often distorted, by campaign opponents.

Rosemary said, "Many thanks, congressman. We really appreciate your help on this."

* * *

MAY 5, 7:30 P.M. -- Gary Wilson had gotten Rep. Mike Oxley to agree to meet with us at the Capitol Hill Club, the Republican club diagonally across the street from the Cannon House Office Building.

We sat in the lounge as Wilson and the congressman reminisced about their times together at Miami of Ohio. Knowing I still had one more visit to make, at 8:30 with staff for Rep. Paul Rogers, I waited until almost eight before breaking into the conversation.

"Congressman," I began, "we'd really like your support in markup tomorrow morning in the Fossil and Synthetic Fuels Subcommittee." I explained the situation, including the critical importance to PPG at Lake Charles. Wilson nodded as Oxley looked over at him.

I started to recount our arguments on the issue, but Oxley stopped me. "You left those papers with us a while ago, and I've seen them. I have no problem backing you guys on this one, okay?"

"Absolutely okay," I replied. "And thanks much."

I left Wilson chatting with Oxley and went upstairs in the club. There was still half an hour before the meeting with Rep. Rogers' staff, and I used part of the time to phone and leave a message for Bob Steder, recounting everything that had taken place this afternoon, what our group was doing this evening, and promising to give him a full report after tomorrow's House subcommittee vote.

* * *

MAY 5, 8:28 P.M. -- The first three meetings had proven easy. This one also figured to be brief and to the point. My contact on the staff was Jeff Schwartz, a casual acquaintance with whom I'd worked on environmental issues a few times. (Schwartz would later be a major drafter of the House version of the Safe Drinking Water Act.)

Rogers was out of the office, so I opted to try for a meeting with Schwartz, even though he was not Rogers' energy legislative assistant, because I knew him and because he was the senior L. A. in the office.

Nevertheless, and as no surprise to me, Schwartz wanted his energy man to be in our meeting. I once again briefly explained the situation; Rogers had seen our arguments, and had seen Texaco's as well.

I explained that Chairman Sharp had indicated his support for our position in a conversation with Walgren, and that we really needed Mr. Rogers to back us on this vote.

"How are you going to visit all eighteen members of the subcommittee before tomorrow's vote?" asked Schwartz.

"We have a team of five or six people doing that," I replied.

"And you personally chose us. My, I am impressed," said Schwartz.

I smiled. "Hey, I chose the cream of the crop."

"Well," said the environmental aide, "we certainly hold no brief for Texaco. And if the residential consumer is protected, as you and George White have told us, I'll reaffirm what the congressman told George White, that you can count on our vote."

I thanked both men and headed to the nearest deli for a sandwich and a cup of coffee before going over to the Rayburn Building and Walgren's office to brief Mary Jo, and then down to the lobby to compare notes with our team.

CHAPTER THIRTY-SEVEN

"A PRETTY GOOD FEELING"

MAY 5, 10:10 P.M. -- I SAT on a marble bench in the South Capitol Street lobby of Rayburn, musing about the breakneck pace of today's activities, and the fact that we had carefully mapped out a short- and long-term strategy, only to see so much come together in one dizzying day.

Foster and I had checked in with Mary Jo, who told us things looked promising. "Bob Cole and Lew Dale called with generally favorable reports."

"No word yet from John Ferguson?"

"Not so far."

"Well, I'll be seeing him along with the others at 10:15 down in the lobby. I'll leave a message for you after we meet."

"Good," Mary Jo had concluded.

* * *

MAY 5, 10:14 P.M. -- Ferguson was first to arrive, followed almost immediately by Cole and Dale, and then Foster and me. We stood in a corner of the nearly empty lobby.

"John," I began, "M.J. told me a few minutes ago she'd heard from Bob and Lew but not from you. So what've you got?"

"Sorry," said Ferguson, "I flat forgot to check in with her. But anyway, here's the deal: the staffers for all three of my guys, Wirth, Markey and Gore, wanted to know where Sharp is on our issue. I didn't want to give away too much, so I said that to the best of my knowledge, he supports us, though I couldn't vouch for that. And incidentally," he added, nodding at Cole, "Bob joined me on the Markey visit."

Ferguson continued, "Gore's guy just smiled at my answer, while the other two asked why I think we have Sharp with us. I told them that's pretty much the word we have from the subcommittee staff, and also mentioned the support from Walgren."

"That's a reasonable answer," I offered. "I took it a bit further with Paul Rogers' staff, but then I know Jeff Schwartz, so I told him that Sharp specifically told Walgren he supports us." This last brought no response from any of the others, so I asked Cole for his report.

"Well, other than the Markey visit, I saw Corcoran; he said you and someone else from PPG had already sold him on the issue." I nodded, and Bob continued, "Slattery's aide said she couldn't commit the congressman without seeing him, and he was at an outside function. I made our case as well as time allowed, and moved on to Don Ritter's office.

"They're not committing, but I got a pretty clear feeling they'll back us. The staffer mentioned that Ritter and Walgren are pretty close … and I hadn't even mentioned Doug Walgren, but I did add, at that point, that Walgren's solidly in our camp."

"Lew?" I asked, turning to Dale.

"I got no concrete positions from Swift's staff. On the other hand, I did see Luken, and while not giving a definite 'yes,' he seemed to lean in our direction."

"Okay," I said. "Broyhill, Madigan and Oxley are all with us, and as I said earlier, I think Rogers will be as well, thanks mainly to that earlier visit by George White."

"Did you see Broyhill, Madigan and Oxley personally?" asked Foster.

I nodded and said, "Yes," then added that it looked like among the members or staffers we saw, there was only one definite "no," several non-committals, with some of those leaning our way, and at least six with us, plus, of course, Sharp and Walgren. "Of course, we figure Hall, Leland and Synar will be with Texaco."

"It might possibly be close, but I have a pretty good feeling about this one," said Foster. "And by the way, I checked in with Bill Simpson at 6:30 and he says Wayne Dowdy will support us as well."

"Ole' Man River does his thing again," I offered, to quizzical looks, then explained the reference to Simpson.

Foster had one final question: "Anybody hear any word that Texaco knows what's coming tomorrow?" All of us shook our heads, and Foster finished with, "It's a good thing nobody went to see Ralph Hall. This is not quite as big a secret as D-Day, but it'll do, it'll do. And now, it's been a long day, and I'm going home to sleep. See you folks tomorrow morning."

I left a message for Zacchero and called it a day.

CHAPTER THIRTY-EIGHT

"THE DEAL WAS CUT"

MAY 6, 9:50 A. M. -- ROSEMARY O'BRIEN had alerted the Second Six, and all ten of us, plus Foster, were gathered in the hallway on the second floor of the Rayburn House Office Building, just outside the subcommittee hearing room.

Nobody from Texaco or the John Camp law firm was in sight. I noted that fact to Foster, and, smiling, he said only, "Amazing. Just amazing."

The markup began shortly after 10. After Mr. Sharp explained the reason for this morning's session, "to begin action on this important measure," he asked if ranking member Ralph Hall of Texas had any opening remarks. Hall spoke briefly and elliptically, leaving many in the room wondering what he meant. The gist was that what was about to happen may or may not be in "regular order" *(in accordance with the usual procedures of the committee)*. He added nothing further, and Chairman Sharp proceeded with the markup, going immediately to our section of the bill.

The subcommittee clerk started to read the section, and Doug Walgren asked for recognition, saying he had an amendment at the desk.

Walgren asked that the clerk read the amendment -- our amendment. He then asked that he be allowed five minutes to explain it.

At that moment, I saw Don Annett of Texaco come into the room, alone and far too late to have an impact unless he had been busy lobbying subcommittee members' offices in hopes of turning a few minds around at the last minute.

Walgren used all of our arguments in speaking for the amendment, focusing on sanctity of contract and on the importance of avoiding dislocations in the natural gas marketplace, then adding a mention of the downstream impact of the products we make, meaning the end-use products in the market place, with all the jobs associated in their manufacture.

Ralph Hall spoke for seven minutes in opposition to the amendment, being allowed an additional two minutes by the chairman upon Hall's request. He recounted all of Texaco's arguments, hitting hardest at what he called "the inequity of a few Louisiana companies benefiting from a sweetheart deal," while ignoring the matter of contract sanctity.

I felt like I was watching the closing arguments on an old Perry Mason TV episode.

Then, at 10:26 a.m. on May 6, the vote was called. Normally, it begins with a voice vote, and then one or more members ask for a "division," meaning a recorded vote.

But Rep. Madigan had known what he was talking about last night. There was a clear voice vote majority in support of the Walgren amendment. And nobody, but *nobody*, asked for a recorded vote!

I looked over at my partners, and every brow was raised except Foster's. Bill whispered to me and Cole, "Obviously, the deal was cut early this morning, between Sharp and Hall. That must've been when Hall alerted Don Annett. I have no idea what tradeoffs between Sharp and Hall might've been involved for other parts of the bill, but let's not worry about that, gentlemen."

The subcommittee markup would continue in the coming days and weeks but we had won another key round in the fight, and the relief was palpable. As we filed out of the room, I looked around for Don Annett, but he had apparently already left.

Foster drove back to Patton Boggs, while Cole, Dale and Ferguson shared a cab ride back to their offices and I headed over to Doug Walgren's office to thank Mary Jo. I would phone Bob Steder immediately after that.

CHAPTER THIRTY-NINE

"CONSTITUENT SERVICE"

MAY 6, 11:12 A.M. -- THIS TIME, I was kept waiting to see Zacchero. Staff director Jon Delano explained only that she had someone in the office with her, and suggested that I wait for a few minutes.

Some fifteen minutes later, M.J. appeared at a door with a bemused look, and motioned me in.

"M.J.," I began, "by now you know we won by voice vote on Doug's amendment." Before I could once again offer our thanks, she nodded and said, "Let me explain why you were kept waiting out here. Don Annett just left my office by the side door, and he was livid."

"I'll bet he was," I said. "So what did you tell him?"

"I just told him it was constituent service. I wound up repeating that several times until he finally stormed out."

"M.J., I've said it before and I'll say it now: you are absolutely the best."

"Thanks, but this is just one more round. You guys still have to watch out during the rest of Sharp's markup, and then there's the full committee over here, plus the Rules Committee before this thing hits the floor, not to mention Senate committee and floor action."

"That we do, and I'll be seeking your good counsel as we move along in the House."

"I'll be here, and do keep me in the loop, but this is your fight, Ed."

I headed back to my office, briefed Gary Wilson and then phoned in that full report I'd promised to Bob Steder. He was more than pleased.

"That's terrific news, man! So where do we go from here?"

"Well, first I need to send a quick note of thanks and congratulations to Foster and the other guys in the First Four, and to copy in the Second Six as well, for what we've achieved so far. Then I'll send an update memo to PPG management, copying you on it. After that, we'll need to have another planning meeting next week, probably with all ten of us and Foster.

"But before that," I continued, "I need a mental health break. Never been happier to see a Friday afternoon roll around. I plan to go home, crash, and sleep 'til noon tomorrow."

"Well, I'll sleep easier tonight; that's for sure," echoed Steder.

CHAPTER FORTY

A WAKE-UP CALL

SUNDAY, MAY 8, 11:30 P.M. -- I HAD turned out the lights twenty minutes earlier and was just falling asleep when the phone next to my bed rang, waking both me and my wife. Groggily, I reached over, picked up the receiver and said, "Hello."

There was a momentary silence on the other end. Then a male voice replied, "Ed, this is George. I'm disappointed."

Not yet fully awake, I replied, "George? George who?"

"You know damn well who, Ed. And I'm really disappointed."

By now I realized the voice on the other end had to be George Tenet, and responded, "George, you did give the senator our full position, right? But we never heard back from you."

There was another pause, followed by the phone being hung up.

"Who was that?" asked Sharon.

"I'm pretty sure it was the energy legislative aide to Senator Heinz."

"What'd he want?"

"I'm not really sure what it was about," I replied, "but it's not worth worrying over." Sharon mumbled something, rolled over on her side and went back to sleep while I stayed awake for about thirty minutes wondering what specific action or actions had triggered Tenet's late-night phone call. Whatever it was, he was obviously upset, and I recalled Bill Foster's caution to us last Thursday night about PPG and Air Products having to work with Senator Heinz in the future.

As sleep once again began to overtake me, I was reminding myself to brief Cole, Dale and Ferguson about this call in the morning.

* * *

MONDAY, MAY 9, 9:55 A. M. -- I first phoned Rosemary O'Brien and Russell King to sound them out about a joint planning meeting. The three of us decided to hold the group meeting on Wednesday at 9:30 in Freeport McMoRan's conference room. I said nothing to either of them about the phone call from Tenet. But I did arrange a conference call with the First Four to fill them in on what had happened last night.

Bob Cole's view was that someone, most likely Senator Heinz himself, must have landed on Tenet. That seemed like a reasonable assumption, but we still weren't sure why. Then Ferguson said, "Maybe I better call my brother-in-law and find out what he wrote in his column. I'll let you know what I learn."

But I didn't have to wait for Ferguson's reply. Five minutes after that call Tena came in and announced, "This is one call you need to take; it's Bob Steder, to debrief you on a call he just had from Mr. Williams," meaning L. Stanton Williams, PPG's CEO and chairman.

"Hey, Bob, so you spoke with the big boss," I began.

"Actually, he called my boss, John Brownell, who as you know is VP of Supply for the company. And John wanted me on the call. Anyway, Mr. Williams asked what we thought about the front page story in yesterday morning's paper out here."

"Uh-oh," I replied. "Front page story? What story? And what'd Williams say next?"

"Well, as he said, the story talked about last week's vote in the Senate Energy Committee, and added that we had won on a tie. I told him that was correct, and he replied, first by saying that's good work on the part of our coalition. But then he added that the story took Senator Heinz to task for not supporting us and Air Products on the vote."

"Was there an editorial on it? I mean, did he say if the paper editorialized?"

"Not really. They just questioned why Heinz wouldn't support us and would back Texaco instead. And they went on to explain a bit about the issue, the fight between our coalition and Texaco over direct sale, not-for-resale contracts."

I was surprised at that. Apparently, Ferguson's brother-in-law had referred the gist of John's phone call to the news staff, and a reporter had done some digging before running the story.

"Bob, how long was the article?"

"I've got it here, now. It's about seven inches. But it was on page one of the Sunday *Pittsburgh Press*."

"Wow," I responded.

"And there's more you should know," added Steder.

"I can hardly wait."

"Right. Williams told us that yesterday afternoon he played tennis with Heinz, and when they were finished and had showered, Heinz mentioned that he assumed Williams would be a leader in his next re-election campaign. Williams told him he wasn't so sure about that, and Heinz seemed genuinely surprised and asked him why not. Williams asked if Heinz had seen the morning newspaper, and Heinz said he'd been working on a speech all morning and hadn't seen the papers yet."

With a fair degree of anxiety, I asked, "So what did Williams say then?"

"He said he told Heinz about the article, and Heinz was perplexed. He said he had talked in general terms with Dexter Baker of Air Products about the issue but that he had made no concrete assurances to him. Then he said he didn't realize PPG was so interested in this one."

"Damn!" I expostulated. "As you well know, Bob, we spoke with his staff two times about it, left them all the position papers, and we were assured that our position would get directly to the senator. And you know that we had tried to meet with Heinz himself but were told he was locked into other meetings, and that was after we had scheduled the second appointment with him specifically." I realized I sounded like I was explaining the situation to Williams himself.

"So what did Williams say?" I continued. "How did he and Heinz leave things?"

"Apparently more or less amicably. Heinz told Williams he'd look into the situation and find out if there had been some sort of mix-up that kept him out of the loop on our position."

That triggered a key question from me: "You never mentioned the call from Tenet, right?"

"Come on, Ed, give me a little credit here. Of course I didn't. Williams asked what our next move would be on the legislation, and I told him you were holding a meeting with all ten companies in the coalition to plan the next steps. He was surprised to hear the coalition was that big. Apparently he thought it was just PPG, Air Products, Kaiser and Georgia Pacific. I couldn't recall all six of the other companies, but at any rate, he didn't seem to mind about that. He finished by saying -- and this is a quote -- 'You guys just be sure our interests are fully protected.'"

"And you said?"

"We told him we would and thanked him for the call."

"Well, you have had a busy morning, my friend. I'll brief Bill Foster and the rest of the First Four. Thanks for keeping my tail out of the sling, Bob. But then again, as somebody I know once said, 'That's what we pay you the big bucks for,' right?"

I hung up the phone and let out a deep, audible breath as Tena peeked in, asking, "What was that all about?"

I gave a thumbs-up and said, "As far as I can tell, it's all good. Come on into Gary's office and we'll see if it's okay with him that I brief both of you at the same time."

Gary Wilson had no problem with the simultaneous briefing, and after I covered the Steder phone call for the two of them, the next call was to Bob Cole. While I was talking to Cole, Tena handed me a "call holding" note. Ferguson was on the other line. I asked her to tell John I'd call him back in a couple of minutes and finished the call to Cole.

Bob's response was succinct: "Jesus, Ed, you seem to enjoy playing in traffic." Then he added, "Are we, that is, you, gonna be able to work with Heinz again in the future?"

"From what Stan Williams told Steder and Brownell, I think we'll be okay with him. It's his staff, particularly Tenet, I'm worried about. From what I can tell, it seems clear the senator may have landed hard on him after talking with Williams." Then, after a moment, I added, "You know what, Bob? It could well be that even if Heinz had known our take on the matter, the best we would've gotten was his abstention from that vote, given his continued objections to the way the whole bill is being written."

"Which would've given us a 9-8 win."

"Yeah, that's true. So either way, we came out okay on this one."

* * *

MAY 9, 10:35 A. M. -- I finished by briefing Cole on the tentative plans for our next meeting of the full group, and immediately called Ferguson.

"Sorry about that, John, I was on the phone with Bob Steder, who'd just been called by Mr. Williams, who told him about the page one article on our issue in yesterday's paper."

"Really? Williams? That likely fits right in with what I learned." John went on to report that his brother-in-law, had, in fact, done just what I had figured from Williams' comments to Steder and his boss, Brownell. I filled John in on the Williams-Heinz tennis date yesterday and its aftermath, including that Heinz told Williams he would "look into" why Heinz hadn't gotten PPG's position.

"So it would seem our man Tenet dropped the ball, right?"

I answered, "Well, as they might say in court, 'facts assumed,' but that seems like a reasonable interpretation. So do you think we should share this with all ten companies, John?"

Ferguson replied, "My first reaction would be to just keep it in the First Four, even though I suspect it's bound to leak out sooner or later. Still, how about we hold it to our four for now, and explain later if need be?"

"That's fine with me."

I told Ferguson about my calls to O'Brien and King and the 9:30 a.m. Wednesday planning meeting, then set up another conference call and explained the Heinz situation, plus the upcoming meeting, to Dale and Bill Foster.

CHAPTER FORTY-ONE

"TODAY'S WALL STREET JOURNAL"

MAY 9, 1:25 P.M. -- ROSEMARY O'BRIEN was back on the phone with me. "Hey, Ed, did you see the Doug Walgren letter to the editor of the *Wall Street Journal* in today's paper?"

I made a mental note to ask that we subscribe to the *Journal*, and said, "Not yet. Why?"

"Well, fish it out and take a look; you're gonna like what you see. It's a really good rebuttal of that *Journal* editorial from last week."

"Excellent. Let's have copies made for Wednesday's meeting."

I hung up the phone and went downstairs to the small shop in the lobby, grabbing their next-to-last copy of the paper. Turning to the "Letters" page, Walgren's message was by far the longest piece. It read, in part:

"...Your editorial unfortunately offers a one-sided view of the controversy over whether natural gas producers should be able to break certain long-term contracts for 'direct sales' to industries... As the author of the amendment unanimously agreed to by the House Subcommittee on Fossil and Synthetic Fuels, I feel that a fair consideration of the issue will show that it would be wrong for the Congress to deny industrial gas consumers and their customers the benefits of these long-term supply contracts.

"Direct sale contracts ... date back to the early 1960's, when certain oil companies were actually flaring unmarketable associated gas from oil wells because they had no market for the gas. These producers sought out certain industries with large natural gas requirements, offering them guaranteed supplies of natural gas at stated prices in return for these industries constructing new plants near the producers' wells." [PPG at Lake Charles had decided to expand our existing facilities based in part on these promises, but now much of the entire facility was dependent on Texaco's direct sale of natural gas.]

The Walgren letter continued, "Both parties were to benefit from this arrangement. The producers gained a secure market for their gas; the industries received assurance of a long-term supply at a guaranteed price. The producers have already substantially realized their benefits, and they now want to withdraw from the arrangement ... If these contracts are broken now, the industries will be left having made literally billions of dollars of investment in reliance on these contracts, but without the benefits bargained for.

"Those seeking to obtain relief for producers from their direct sale contract obligations have unfortunately confused the issue of contract abrogation with the issue of price decontrol. ...

"The legislation being considered by the Congress is an attempt to respond to the many problems in the contracts between pipeline companies and producers that were agreed to during the supply panic of the 1970's. Direct sale contracts are a different matter altogether. Breaking these contracts would do nothing to encourage new development or increase supplies for the nation.

"While it is true that, as the *Journal* editorial points out, most of the direct sale gas is sold in a few southeastern states, the benefits of the direct sales are shared by the entire nation. The industrial purchasers of the direct sale gas manufacture the fertilizer used on our farms and the petrochemicals and aluminum used in the nation's heavy industry. Preservation of their gas supply contracts will help to keep American industry competitive and our workers employed. In contrast, the only beneficiaries of contract abrogation will be the oil companies which will receive the unanticipated -- and unfair -- windfall of being allowed to break contract obligations."

The mention of fertilizers ahead of petrochemicals and aluminum gave me the clue. I phoned back to Rosemary and, taking a shot not quite in the dark, said, "Congratulations; your people did a great job working with Doug on the response. It hit all the right points, and hit them hard."

Rosemary laughed and said, "So you figured it out. How'd you do that?"

I explained and she laughed again. "So anyway, you liked the letter, eh?"

"Absolutely. And please do bring extra copies for all of us on Wednesday."

"Will do," Rosemary promised.

CHAPTER FORTY-TWO

LIBERALS, CONSERVATIVES ... AND OTHERS

MAY 11, 9:30 A.M. -- WE WERE all gathered around the conference table at Freeport McMoRan.

After we congratulated Rosemary on the Walgren letter, and before we began planning our next steps, Bill Foster spoke up: "I thought you might like to know what we learned about Don Nickles' vote for our position last week."

I responded, "You bet."

"We still don't have the specifics, but it seems Nickles had chits out with several other petroleum companies with major facilities in Oklahoma, and those folks weren't eager to see Texaco getting a competitive edge in the form of a three-plus-billion-dollar windfall."

"So they actually convinced Nickles to vote against the Texaco position on this one?" Russell King asked.

"That's the way it looks, though as I said, we still don't have all the specifics."

"Well, it's good enough for us, right?" I noted. Heads were nodding in agreement. "So what's our next step in this dance?"

Foster responded, "I'm doing some checking with Energy Committee staff in the Senate to get an idea for when their markup might end and when they think the bill might reach the floor. From what I get from committee staff, that might not happen any time soon."

"And it'd be a good idea if Ed could check with Walgren as to when the Sharp subcommittee figures to finish its markup and send the bill to full committee," added O'Brien.

"I'd figure that to come up before the Senate acts," offered Russell King.

"Possibly," said Foster, "but I would never place bets on which house of Congress will move first on a bill; just too many variables."

"Okay," I chimed in, "but shouldn't we be talking with House Energy and Commerce members now, while we wait? I mean, we don't want to find ourselves having to repeat last Thursday night's scramble."

"Doing that now might be awfully early, Ed. Still, if you're thinking about putting in placeholders, I'd say go ahead," said Foster. "But there may be an easier and better way to go about this. I'm thinking we can have the same results as going to see almost all members of the committee if we just focus our efforts on Dingell and the key member of each of those four categories that Mary Jo Zacchero suggested to us last Thursday."

Most of the Second Six members looked puzzled, so Foster asked me to explain Mary Jo's idea about dividing our earlier efforts among conservative Republicans, moderate Republicans, moderate Democrats and liberal Democrats. As I finished my explanation, Foster added, "My point here is that all we may really need to do, at least for now, is identify and focus on the key committee member in each of those four categories, plus Mr. Dingell."

"Well, that would be easier," said Rosemary O'Brien. "But Bill, do you guys know who those four are?"

Cole spoke up: "I'd say for the moderate Dems, we have to use Doug Walgren. He's already proven his value in dealing with the subcommittee chairman, and he may be able to work with Sharp in leveraging Dingell as well. I know I can use his help in that department. And Bill, can I assume Bill O'Hara of Patton Boggs will also work with us on lining up Mr. Dingell?"

Foster nodded, adding, "I'd expect that to be the case."

"And since Mr. Broyhill is ranking on the Sharp subcommittee," I added, "I'd say he's the logical guy for me to go back to and see if we can leverage him to gain support from the conservative Republicans on the full committee, right?"

Russell King replied, "You took the words from my mouth on that one, Ed."

That left the moderate Republicans and the liberal Democrats. "We seem to be focusing on guys from within the Sharp subcommittee, and I guess that makes sense, since they've been closest to the situation, know the most about the bill and will likely have the lead in carrying it into full committee," I said.

Lew Dale added, "And don't forget that the subcommittee passed this thing by voice vote with little dissent, despite Doug Walgren's writing that the vote was unanimous, so these guys shouldn't be uncomfortable speaking to their peers on the full committee."

"Yeah," replied O'Brien, "but then again, the voice vote protected them from being recorded on the issue. I'm not so sure they'll want to take the lead at this point."

"Fair point," I conceded, "but the only way to find out is to ask." Turning to the full group, I followed with, "Who are the right members to see for these last two groups, people?"

Russell King spoke first. "I'd say Tom Corcoran of Illinois for the moderate Republicans. He's got the respect of his moderate brethren, and he agreed quickly to support us in the subcommittee, right, Ed?" King knew that Phil Pulizzi of PPG and I had met with Corcoran.

"Okay," I said. "Anybody else have another view?"

"Well, there's Don Ritter from Pennsylvania," answered Lew Dale. "But I have no problem with Corcoran, and if it comes to that, I can always go back and ask for Ritter's help as well."

"Okay," said Foster. "So what about the liberal Democrats?"

Nobody spoke up quickly, perhaps not surprising in a gathering of corporate lobbyists. But Bob Cole was reading my mind as he said, "Whoever we choose, we'll need to emphasize that Phil Sharp is with us on this one, so it may not matter all that much which member we try." Then Cole added, "But how about either Paul Rogers of Florida or Tim Wirth of Colorado?"

King spoke up: "Wirth may have some involvement with the oil shale industry in his state, and that may or may not make a difference, but I suspect Rogers would be the better choice."

Foster agreed, adding, "And Rogers is second in line for an environmental subcommittee chairmanship, so he may have a bit more clout than Wirth in this case. Ed, you lined up Rogers' support earlier."

"Not so much me as George, here," I responded.

White said, "Ah think ah can get Rogers to take the lead with the liberals. Would you like to come with me, Ed?"

"George," I answered, "your effectiveness with the Florida delegation is way better than mine. I'm happy to leave Rogers to you."

"Good," said King. "So again, when should we make our contacts?"

"There's no rush," offered Foster. "I don't expect either body of Congress to act on the bill within the next month at least, and maybe not before the July 4th recess. But let's just go ahead and make our placeholder contacts next week, okay?"

"Whoa!" I exclaimed. "You really don't see any more action on this thing for several weeks?"

"They could always surprise us, Ed," Bill answered. "But no. Both houses have full legislative agendas, so even assuming the full committee in the Senate and Sharp's House subcommittee move quickly on the bill, which I doubt they'll do, why would the Senate floor leadership or, for that matter, John Dingell, want to bring up what looks to be a contentious issue before the dust settles?"

King joined in with, "What you're saying also suggests to me that Texaco will be out stirring the pot in the House and Senate during that time."

"Of course," Foster responded. "That's why I'm saying it's okay to reinforce our contacts next week. Look, Texaco's already lost in full committee in the Senate and subcommittee in the House, and while we certainly need to stay vigilant, I think they'll have a hard time reversing either of those votes. Plus, they've played their card in the press, planting that *Wall Street Journal* editorial, and Rosemary and Walgren did an excellent job of rebutting that one. They may try to get other media contacts on their side, and as I said, we do need to be alert to all of that. But I just don't see any further legislative action in the short term."

With that, we adjourned the meeting, and I was thinking that all of us would have a chance to turn to other issues, for now at least.

CHAPTER FORTY-THREE

CREATING A COLLOQUY

JUNE 15 -- IT HAD been exactly five weeks since the last meeting of the full ten-company coalition. We had made our follow-up visits with leaders in the House Energy and Commerce Committee's Fossil and Synthetic Fuels Subcommittee, and had received assurances that when the time came, they would help us get our message to full committee members. Most important, indications from Cole and Bill O'Hara were that Chairman John Dingell would have no problem supporting us. Not a rock-solid commitment, but as good as we could have expected.

Meanwhile, in the Senate, things had remained at a standstill. The natural gas decontrol bill was still locked in the full committee, and Bill Foster had confirmed that Senator Johnston saw little chance of action until at least after the July 4th recess.

Foster had also checked back with the DOE's Danny Boggs, who had reaffirmed the Reagan administration's strong desire for decontrolling natural gas in the marketplace. Then, however, Boggs had confirmed our earlier suspicions by signaling to Foster his feeling that the multiple amendments in the Senate bill might mean it would take longer to decontrol the price of natural gas than the initial version from the administration.

In Foster's conference call with the First Four, Bob Cole had picked up on that report immediately. "With all the changes the bill has gone through in both houses, do you think that means DOE support for the bill may be softening?" he asked Foster.

Foster had replied, "I don't know for sure, but it does look like some sort of a crack in their solid wall of support for the legislation."

For the first time, I had begun to believe the overall legislation might just die a slow and quiet death, at least for 1983. Under the usual procedures in Congress, that would mean consideration of the bill could be picked up the following year in either house, in theory without losing a step from the current markups. Next year, 1984, would be the second and last year of the 98th Congress. And, also in theory, if the bill failed to pass next year, everything would have to begin anew in the 99th Congress in 1985, meaning we might have to face this fight all over again, a prospect I would not relish.

* * *

JUNE 15, 2 P.M. -- Given these concerns and uncertainty, I had spoken with Foster and Cole and decided to call a meeting of the First Four at PPG. The agenda included a brief review of where we stood in the House and Senate, and then a lengthier look at our next steps and at what Texaco might be planning.

I started the discussion with, "It still seems unlikely to me that this thing will stay dormant all year. DOE wants a bill, even if not in this exact form. The president has emphasized *his* support for it. The Republicans control the Senate, though not the House. So" -- I looked at Foster -- "don't you think they'll find a way to get the bill through Senate Energy and move it to the floor?"

Bill looked at me and smiled. "Well, Ed, the reasons you give are valid. In theory. But this is real life, not theory. Assuming the bill does get through full committee, McClure and Johnston, and especially McClure as chairman of the committee, don't want to have an omelet on their face by bringing a contentious bill to the floor only to see it fail. So I'd say we'd best just sit tight for now. Besides, let's not take our eyes off the prize. If there's no change in the law, everyone in this room is a winner. You guys get to keep your existing long-term contracts with Texaco, and that's a solid win, right?"

I had to agree, adding, "And it's obviously way too early to think about what might happen next year."

"That it is," said Foster.

"So," I continued, "let's turn to what our friends at Texaco might be thinking. Anyone have any intel on their activity?"

Cole, Dale and Ferguson were silent, then Foster said, "I've been thinking about how natural gas is extracted, and wondering whether Texaco might just want to try to carve out an approach that would work to their benefit."

"Whaddya mean?" I asked.

"I'm talking about something -- two somethings, actually -- called tertiary recovery and infill drilling."

"What's that?" asked Cole.

Foster explained. "It can get highly technical, but basically, tertiary recovery is any enhanced natural gas recovery process that goes beyond the use of gas recycling or water flooding in an effort to increase production. And infill drilling involves drilling additional wells within the pool of natural gas, to increase the productive capacity of the pool. It can also involve drilling between existing wells for the same purpose."

Dale asked, "And Texaco's point would be ... what?"

"Their point might be to try to find sponsors to help them craft language that would cover the additional reserves of gas brought to the surface in these ways, and let that gas be sold at the January 1, 1985, market price or at whatever price exists when the complete bill is signed into law. They would reason that these are new reserves of gas and thus shouldn't be included in the terms of your existing contracts with Texaco."

"That wouldn't amount to a whole lot of gas, though, would it?" asked Ferguson. "I mean, would it even be worth the effort for them to try that approach?"

"Well, put yourself in Texaco's place, and especially in Don Annett's place." answered Foster. "You've been beaten at every turn so far, and who knows exactly how much more gas these approaches might yield? Wouldn't you be thinking it's at least worth a try?"

"Maybe so," Ferguson offered. "So how would we deal with this situation, if they act on it?"

Foster had a ready answer: "When and if the bill gets to the floor, one way, not the best but a good start, would be to beat them to the punch by arranging for an early floor colloquy in the Senate, a colloquy in which, let's say, Johnston asks chairman McClure a question, something like, 'I ask my distinguished committee chairman if it is his understanding, with regard to natural gas decontrol, that gas brought to the surface by enhanced recovery methods such as tertiary recovery and infill drilling would be treated in the same manner as natural gas in existing contracts with regard to contract obligations?'"

I was smiling at the legal-eagle language Foster had concocted. He continued, "And Mr. McClure would respond with something like, 'My esteemed colleague from Louisiana is exactly right in his interpretation of any changes to the language in that section of the natural gas decontrol bill.'"

"And of course, the colloquy would come up only if the legislation reaches the Senate floor," Foster repeated.

"Well," offered Cole, "I yield to your knowledge of the industry. And even though a floor colloquy is pretty far down the list in importance when it comes to legislation, if you think this might be Texaco's next approach, I'm assuming Patton Boggs would arrange for the language in the colloquy, right?"

"Right," answered Foster. "But of course, we … and I mean Patton Boggs … would also develop counter-arguments to any Texaco position on these things, just as I suspect Sara Schotland and outside counsel for some of your other firms would do. Still, Bob, colloquies can be a useful way to clarify the intent of a provision."

"So, what do you guys think about doing that?" I asked.

"I think we need to cover all our bases, and this is one more step in doing that," said Cole.

"Seems reasonable to me," replied Dale.

Ferguson added, "There may be other moves up Texaco's sleeve, but for now, this is one we could at least mitigate. Let's do it, and let's be aware that they still might try to put this tertiary recovery and infill drilling language into the Senate Energy Committee markup or into the Sharp subcommittee markup, or, for that matter, into the committee report."

I nodded to Foster, who replied, "That's why we need to stay tight with the committee staffs on both sides of the Hill."

With that, the meeting adjourned.

* * *

The next afternoon, Foster called to tell me he had vetted the idea of the colloquy with both Senators McClure and Johnston and had written it, using the same wording he had suggested yesterday afternoon. Unless Texaco came up with any surprises, there was nothing to do but sit tight and wait.

CHAPTER FORTY-FOUR

"YOUR JOB AND MINE"

JULY 20, 9:40 A.M. -- MORE THAN a month had gone by, with the legislation still stuck in House subcommittee, and Senate Energy having held three more markup sessions after the 4th of July recess. Foster called to tell me a Patton Boggs paralegal would attend today's markup, just as their staff had covered the other three with nothing meaningful to report.

Today would be different.

As *The Wall Street Journal* reported the next morning, "Western Republicans combined with Democrats from gas-producing states to narrowly defeat a major challenge to natural gas decontrol legislation in the Senate Energy Committee."

The *Journal* report continued: "The vote appears to clear the way for final committee approval of a producer-oriented decontrol bill in the next few days. But even the bill's staunchest supporters concede that it faces a tough fight in the full Senate and is likely to be challenged by lawmakers from gas-consuming states.

"By a 9-9 vote," (a margin familiar to our group), "a bipartisan coalition supporting decontrol thwarted attempts to restore to the bill many of the free-market principles and consumer protection measures originally proposed by the Reagan administration."

The article continued, recounting the "months of debate and hard lobbying in the committee" and saying that it "generally goes further than the White House advocated in allowing rates to rise over the next few years. The committee approved in principle a complex decontrol timetable requiring the renegotiation of most existing contracts, a phasing out of all federal price controls by 1987 and the imposition of a temporary price cap during the transition period.

"Sen. John Heinz (R.-Pa), one of the lawmakers who pledged to try to block the bill on the Senate floor, asserted that it includes 'an offensive double standard.' He said that 'if decontrol is good for the country it's good for the country' and that the 'special interest provisions' should be eliminated. Sen. John Melcher (D.-Mont.), another opponent, argued that the bill 'is extremely vulnerable, because it allows large amounts of intrastate gas to remain at artificially low prices, sometimes less than 10 percent of free market prices.'

"Opponents hoped to break up the coalition behind the bill by requiring uniform treatment and a single nationwide definition of specific categories of gas. If that amendment had passed, Sen. Bennett Johnston (D.- La) and several other backers almost certainly would have withdrawn their support and the legislation would have died....

"But the coalition held firm under the leadership of Sen. James McClure (R.-Id.), the committee's chairman. He made it clear that the Republican majority is willing to accept the controversial provisions in exchange for essential Democratic votes supporting the entire package."

Well, now. There were a few affirmations and a worrying-point tucked into the *Journal* report. For one, the part about requiring the renegotiation of most existing contracts jumped out at me. I hadn't focused closely enough on the full bill -- we had Patton Boggs and Sara Schotland for that -- to realize that with the help of Foster and his staff as well as Schotland, our coalition had in fact carved out what might have been a single key exemption from the overall approach of the bill.

But then there was the quote from John Heinz. Clearly, he was still opposed, and not just to the way the entire bill was being written, but also to the sort of exemption we had gained. I wondered now if he would, in fact, have absented himself from the vote on our specific amendment had he known the impact on PPG.

I phoned Foster and asked first if he had seen the report. "Of course," came the reply.

"Well. It drives home the job you and we did on this baby."

"Yes. But it probably goads John McKinley of Texaco to push even harder with Annett to try to work some magic and get our win reversed. I don't see it happening; I'm just saying we need to be on our toes." That oft-repeated caution by Foster had proved to be wise counsel so far.

"Bill, there's another thing," I offered. "Reading that piece this morning made me wonder about how solid the consumer protection provision in our amendment is when you look at the whole bill."

"I don't follow you."

"Well, our fix is solely for 'not for resale' intrastate natural gas. The bill is far broader than that."

"Ed, we focused on what we were supposed to focus, the 'not for resale' language. That's the provision that Bennett, with McClure and Ford, put in and that protected us."

"I get that," I replied. "It's just that we might lose a major talking point in both houses if this thing doesn't also protect the consumer of interstate as well as intrastate gas."

"Look, Ed. First off, your job and mine is to protect your interests. Second, I'm not sure the consumer isn't protected as well. Don't forget, twenty-four states have intrastate gas."

"Maybe," I answered. "But when all is said and done, I'm not gonna be too disappointed if the entire bill fails."

"And that may happen, Ed. As we all know, it's extremely contentious, in many ways."

CHAPTER FORTY-FIVE

A SENATE SURPRISE

JULY 26, 3:40 P.M. -- SINCE FOSTER'S phone call last week, I had begun attending the Senate Energy Committee markups, mainly to be sure Texaco was pulling no surprises but partly out of curiosity to see if and when the bill would make it to the Senate floor. Patton Boggs had a paralegal at the markups as well.

The debate had been contentious all week, and anyone could see that Chairman McClure's patience was wearing thin. At 2:40 p.m. he had called for a vote on a particularly controversial amendment, one to delete a provision that would lift price controls from *all* gas discovered before 1977, so-called "old gas." That amendment had failed on an 11-8 vote, and it seemed to McClure that the committee was hopelessly deadlocked on the overall bill.

At 3:10 p.m., the chairman had called a five-minute recess while he huddled with Johnston and Ford, plus Senators Mark Hatfield of Oregon and Connecticut Senator Lowell Weicker and senior committee staff. As is usually the case with "five-minute recesses" in congress, the break lasted thirty minutes.

Now, McClure gaveled the committee back to order and announced a highly unusual decision. "The ranking minority member and I have decided to ask the committee for a vote to send this measure to the Senate floor without recommendation."

I looked over at the press table, where reporters were frantically writing in their notepads and checking their tape recorders. As for me, I was buffaloed, never having seen this tactic before in the Senate or, for that matter, in the House. Bills are passed or defeated in committee. Certain Senate committees, in their "advise and consent" role, might conceivably send a nomination to the floor without recommendation -- for example, after a contentious hearing on a Supreme Court nominee -- but the Energy Committee seemed to be setting a precedent with this action by punting a piece of legislation to the Senate floor.

At any rate, the vote began at 3:40 p.m. and ended at 3:48. The result was 11-9 to do as Chairman McClure had requested.

As *The Washington Post* would report the next morning, "The vote became possible when ... Hatfield ... and Weicker agreed to report the bill out without a recommendation of approval, according to committee Chairman James A. McClure ... .

"Three Democrats joined with eight Republicans in voting for the action.

"Though the bill would retain price controls longer than the Reagan administration version, Energy Secretary Donald P. Hodel termed it 'a step in the right direction' and expressed hope for Senate passage early in September.

"But McClure, who yesterday noted that the committee had spent 'a nearly unprecedented amount of time marking up the bill,' seemed more relieved than encouraged by his panel's action.

" 'As long and as tough as this step has been, the next one's tougher,' he said. 'And assuming we get a bill passed on the floor, I think ultimate agreement between the Senate and House is even tougher.'"

The *Post* article continued, "McClure said that while he expected the legislation to reach the floor sometime in the fall he had not obtained 'any specific commitments' from Senate Majority Leader Howard H. Baker (R-TN).... ."

So, with Congress leaving in the next few weeks for its month-long August recess, it was apparent that in the Senate at least, there would be no further action on the bill until September and quite possibly later than that.

It was time for me to do several things: update Bob Steder, send a memo to PPG management, check in with Russell King and Rosemary O'Brien, and set up a meeting with the First Four and maybe all ten companies to review the bidding.

CHAPTER FORTY-SIX

"WHY DIDN'T WE KNOW?"

JULY 27, 8 A.M. -- I WALKED into my office to find a long *Pittsburgh Press* article lying front and center on my desk. Tena had gotten to work early and sorted the mail and overnight fax traffic from PPG headquarters. This article had been faxed by Bob Steder. What had caught her eye was the pullout quote at the top of columns three and four of the six-column article: "We know there are some companies in Pennsylvania that are going to get hurt. But we're trying to make this thing as unattractive as possible because the bill's so bad."

The quote was attributed to "George Tenet, aide to Senator Heinz."

Apparently, Ferguson's call to his brother-in-law had alerted the newspaper's staff -- in particular, reporter Kathy Kiely -- to follow the issue closely. Eyes widening, I sat down and began to read: "When it comes to the big fight over natural gas prices and how high they should be allowed to rise, Sen. John Heinz thinks he knows what's best for Pennsylvania customers.

"Rep. Doug Walgren thinks he does too.

"So why are the two Pittsburgh [members of Congress] -- both of whom hold key positions to help determine levels of one of the most basic costs of living for the foreseeable future -- on opposite sides of the same issue?

"The reasons may be sinister and fraught with special interests. On the other hand, it may all boil down to a simple difference of opinion and tactics.

"One thing is certain, however. The battle over the natural gas bill being readied for review by Congress has become so complicated no one will be able to sort out all the motives of the elected officials who have their hands on it.

"....Last week's split between Heinz, the state's senior Republican senator, and Walgren, a Democrat from Mt. Lebanon" [a Pittsburgh suburb] "merely serves to dramatize the confusion existing in the debate over natural gas deregulation.

".... Take the matter that divided the two Pennsylvanians. The gas deregulation proposals being considered in Congress would do two major things: they would get the government out of the business of setting the price of the valuable household and industrial commodity, and [they would] leave gas producers almost free to charge what the market will bear."

The article went on to describe arcane provisions in the legislation that would affect Gulf Oil Corporation, which at that time was still an oil giant based in Pittsburgh, in its dealings with Texas Eastern Pipeline, a major gas supplier to the Northeast. It turns out that Texas Eastern had negotiated an agreement with Gulf in the 1960's, an agreement similar to the one our coalition members had with Texaco. And as the reporter noted, "Natural gas goes for about $2.50 to $3.00 a thousand cubic feet today."

The article continued, "Gulf would like to get out of the arrangement, which is not due to expire until the end of the decade. Gulf has tried unsuccessfully to do so in a case that went all the way to the Supreme Court. Now it looks as though Congress may make it possible for Gulf to do what the courts would not allow.

"....[Walgren introduced] an amendment to the House gas deregulation bill that would make a special exception in the contract abrogation clause for Texas Eastern and several other firms. Among those are two Pennsylvania manufacturers, PPG Industries of Pittsburgh and Air Products Co. of Allentown.

"Both firms make petrochemicals at Louisiana plants. Both use gas as a fuel and raw material. Both have long-term contracts, signed in the 1960's, which will enable them to get gas at a bargain rate well into this decade.

"....Walgren argued his amendment was in the consumers' interest. Most of his colleagues on the subcommittee drafting the House gas deregulation bill agreed, approving the measure with so little acrimony they didn't even take a roll call vote."

Hey, I thought, if the reporter wants to make it sound that straightforward and simple, I'm all for that, even if she had mischaracterized the principal reason for Doug Walgren's amendment.

The article continued, "In the Senate committee, things were different. Bennett Johnston, a Democrat from Louisiana, where most of the companies that benefit from bargain gas are located, had written into the Senate bill a provision protecting them."

The story went on to explain that Heinz had opposed the Johnston amendment, "to the chagrin of PPG and Air Products executives, many of whom had contributed heavily to his re-election campaign ... .

"Johnston reportedly offered to expand his exemption provision to take care of the Texas Eastern Pipeline contract if Heinz and fellow Northeasterners Bill Bradley, D-NJ., and Lowell Weicker, R-CT, would drop their opposition to the exemptions he wanted.

"Heinz would have none of it. His legislative aide, George Tenet, explained that the senator is so opposed to the gas decontrol proposals being considered that he doesn't want to do anything that might make them vaguely palatable.

DODGING THE BULLET

" .... Like most senators from the region, Heinz doesn't buy the Reagan administration's argument that allowing gas producers to charge what the market will bear will result in more gas being produced, and hence, lower prices.

"Tenet says Heinz intends to fight against decontrol on the Senate floor and will use the Johnston exemptions -- which he failed by a 9-9 vote to have knocked out of the Senate bill -- as ammunition. Heinz intends to argue that allowing some gas contracts to be broken and others to stand would be inequitable and unfair, even though in making that argument he will be working against the interests of some of his more prominent constituents.

" 'We know there are some companies in Pennsylvania that are going to get hurt,' Tenet said. 'We know about PPG and Air Products. But we're trying to make this thing as unattractive as possible because the bill's so bad.'

"... Isn't it possible that Gulf executives, who gave even more money to the Heinz campaign than their PPG counterparts did, influenced Heinz in his decision to reject the quid pro quo Johnston offered?

" 'Oh, no,' said Tenet. 'They've been perfect gentlemen.'"

Well, now, I thought. First off, credit Ms. Kiely with a good sense of irony for the line she used to finish the piece. Could it really have been as simple a matter as Gulf having outspent PPG and Air Products? And if so, how did we, and Bill Foster, fail to discover Gulf's major role in the issue? Both I and the people at headquarters might have some questions to answer, as might Lew Dale.

I had smiled, while reading the article, at the reporter's naiveté in explaining what triggered Senator Johnston's amendment, but that was just as well. It's best for Washington reps not to be part of the story as it unfolds.

At the same time, there were more important issues here: the article explained and clarified a couple of things. First, now we could be pretty sure what Heinz's motives were in opposing us in that Energy Committee 9-9 vote, even if campaign contributions were not the tipping point. And, I speculated, we also might have the reason for Tenet's not wanting us to speak directly with Heinz. I would sound out Lew Dale first thing, but my view, for now at least, was that Tenet was protecting his boss, albeit we would have preferred it if he had been willing to let us make the case directly with Heinz. But then, I reasoned, Tenet may have figured that after Dale and I failed in our attempt to gain Heinz's support, we would have our CEO's call him. It seemed clear now that those efforts would have also been for nothing, and maybe Tenet wanted to shield the senator from those calls.

At any rate, I reckoned, we need to get the First Four and Foster together, to mull over our next steps in light of the broader picture presented in the article. I knew the legislation was extremely complex, but now, perhaps, we needed to adjust our sights, and -- remembering what Foster had said about keeping our eyes on the prize -- just wait quietly and hope the entire bill goes down.

* * *

I was on the phone with Lew Dale.

"I know, I know," he began. "The article was just read to me over the phone from Allentown. So now we know why Tenet wouldn't let us see Heinz, don't you think?"

"Sounds as if you and I read the piece the same way, or at least, you got the same view from listening to it. Be sure they're sending it to you ASAP."

"That's being done. But let me ask you, why didn't we know about Gulf Oil's role in all of this?"

"Lew, we're thinking exactly the same way. I'll get with Bob Steder. It was he who sent me the article. Somebody, he or we, should've seen this coming. And come to think of it, Mary Jo, as good as she is, had never told us about Walgren offering to weigh in on the Gulf-Texas Eastern fight."

Dale hadn't carried it quite that far, likely because Air Products was based in Allentown, while we and Gulf were in Pittsburgh. If so, he had a point, and I chose not to press the matter.

"In any event, how about we have an August 1 meeting in my office? We may just want to think about changing our plans."

"What do you mean?"

"Well, I was thinking we might just want to sit back, quietly, and watch the bill fail. After all, Bill Foster hit that point the other day; if the law stays the same, we're okay."

"That may be true, Ed, but I seriously doubt the other folks in our group would want to see all their hard work count for nothing, and I know most major corporations really want to see this thing pass."

"Even so," I countered, "the last thing Mr. Williams said to Bob Steder was to be sure our interests are protected, and I'm sure Mr. Baker feels the same way."

"In any event," Dale concluded, "it might be a subject for us all to discuss."

The next call was to Steder. "Interesting article, no?" Bob asked.

"That's one way to look at it, but yeah, it was interesting, and it certainly clarifies the reason for Heinz's vote, and maybe for Tenet's actions as well."

"I'm with you on Heinz, but how does it explain what Tenet did to you guys?"

I offered Bob my reasoning, adding that one obvious part of any staff person's job is to protect the boss. Bob responded with, "I guess I understand that. But aren't you guys still ticked at the way Tenet blew you off?"

"I'd have appreciated it if he'd been candid with us, that's for sure. But let me ask you, Bob, did you know anything about Gulf's contracts for natural gas?"

"Honestly, I didn't," Steder answered, "just as I guess you didn't know that their lobbyists were working on Heinz."

"True," I admitted. "They didn't even leave footprints in their lobbying. But then, we did win in Senate Energy, and I'd say that's the most important thing to our management, wouldn't you agree?"

"Absolutely."

* * *

The call to Bill Foster was brief. Foster had not seen the *Pittsburgh Press* piece and wanted to reserve judgment until he had read it. His only comment when I mentioned being surprised at the Gulf Oil role in the legislation was, "Yeah, it looks as if that caught *all of us* by surprise."

"True, that." I replied.

CHAPTER FORTY-SEVEN

"KEEP THAT THOUGHT TO OURSELVES"

AUGUST 1, 10 A.M. -- FOSTER JOINED Cole, Dale, Ferguson and me in a brief review session at PPG. We were to meet tomorrow with the Second Six, upstairs in Freeport's conference room.

Before we turned to trying to dope out what Texaco might do next, Foster said, "I've heard no further word from Sharp on the subcommittee markup schedule or when they hope to finish."

I offered a suggestion: "How about I call either Jim Broyhill, the ranking member on the subcommittee, or Mike Boland, the minority counsel and Broyhill's man on the subcommittee staff?"

"Couldn't hurt." replied Foster. "Do it today, so you can report back at tomorrow's meeting."

With that, we turned to Texaco. Foster reported that from what he could determine, Don Annett and company had not approached any Senate members or staffers about using tertiary recovery or infill drilling as a way to charge the full going rate for at least some of the natural gas supply going to us.

That, of course, was good news, and on balance, perhaps not

surprising. I was musing that maybe our bunch was getting a bit neurotic over what our high-powered opponent and their star attorney might be hatching. Foster had quickly disabused me of that feeling. "Don't think for one minute," he had advised, "that those guys are gonna roll over on this. There's just too much money at stake for that to happen."

As it happened, and as we learned later, Foster's caution was well taken.

* * *

AUGUST 2, 9:30 A.M. -- King kicked off today's meeting. "Seems to me the main thing we need to discuss is any feedback we've received about when Sharp's subcommittee plans to resume marking up the bill. Then we can noodle over the timing in the Senate."

That was my signal to report. Except there was really nothing definitive to say. I had spoken with Mike Boland, who told me that chairman Sharp had advised Mr. Broyhill that he had no idea when his panel might conclude or even resume their markup. Boland had added that there was a backlog of other legislation awaiting action in the subcommittee. I had asked him if that meant the natural gas bill "would be back-burnered" or, to the contrary, that Sharp wanted to speed things up in order to get to those other bills.

"I've no idea at this point," Boland had answered.

"Okay," said Russell King, "then let's look at the Senate floor." Foster looked as if he was about to speak, then settled back and said nothing. I knew he wanted us to take a look at what our opponent might be doing.

It didn't take long for Foster to have his chance. The situation in the Senate was still static. King and Cole had each checked separately with Majority Leader Baker and others in the Senate leadership in both parties and had received the same answer: no action on the bill in the near future.

Then Cole added what was perhaps the most telling bit, "It sounded to me as if they're looking at holding off until next year."

A couple of attendees expressed surprise, and Foster spoke up. "Did they actually say that, Bob, or was that what you took from the meeting?"

"Not their exact words, but I got the clear impression they'd like to avoid a potential bloodbath on the floor as long as possible."

King said, "It might be helpful to know how hard the administration is willing to push the Senate at this point."

"Good point," replied Foster. "I'll check with Danny Boggs and let you guys know."

"Now then," King asked, "should we talk about Texaco's next move? Anybody have any new info?"

Nobody knew of any firm news. Foster shot a glance at me, holding up three fingers. It took a moment, but I realized he wanted to discuss tertiary recover and infill drilling with the full group. I shrugged my shoulders in a "Why not?" gesture, and Bill briefly outlined what tertiary recovery and infill drilling meant. He then explained his plan for a floor colloquy, adding that both Johnston and McClure had approved using the tactic if necessary, as well as Foster's suggested wording.

"Suppose Texaco raises this approach in the House, either in the subcommittee or the full committee?" asked Rosemary O'Brien.

"They might do that," replied Foster, "but I'd think they'd be more likely to try to get an amendment to add the language on the Senate floor, since that would be farther along the track to passage."

O'Brien nodded, and no one else spoke. I took the opportunity to raise the point I'd mentioned earlier with Lew Dale. "You know, this thing is dragging along so slowly that I was wondering how we in this room would feel if the legislation just fails to pass. I mean, all our contracts with Texaco would still be protected, right?"

Russell King looked at me in what I took to be surprise, and said, "That's something a few of us may have considered, but if we want to keep our credibility with the administration, with McClure and Johnston and even with the business community as a whole, I'd suggest we keep that thought to ourselves." It was a valid argument.

King concluded the meeting with, "Well, let's all stay in touch, people. As for myself, I'm going on vacation while Congress is in recess this month. You guys could use a break too."

CHAPTER FORTY-EIGHT

TEXACO REACHES OUT TO STOCKHOLDERS

SEPTEMBER 10, 8:15 A.M. -- I WAS going through the morning mail when Tena handed me an envelope from Rosemary O'Brien. The cover note said simply, "Here's the latest from our friends."

It was a letter from John R. McKinley, chairman and CEO of Texaco, to their stockholders, dated September 9, 1983. It began by telling shareholders the company needed "your help in support of legislation before the Congress to deregulate producer natural gas prices."

The letter told its readers that the "lowest prices to natural gas producers under regulation are for so-called 'old gas.' Your company, as an early supplier of natural gas .... is particularly disadvantaged by having large volumes of its natural gas sales artificially classified as 'old gas.'"

McKinley's last point referred to the fact that gas produced before 1977 was known as "old gas." And yet, to my knowledge, none of Texaco's lobbying efforts had been aimed at changing that designation.

The letter continued, "This gas regulation is restraining Texaco to less than one-tenth the price other producers receive under newer contracts for the same identical commodity. [Apparently, McKinley and his writers chose to ignore Gulf Oil's situation.] No such arbitrary price distinction exists for any other petroleum product.

"The U. S. Senate is expected to vote this fall on a bill which would provide phased deregulation of all natural gas and thereby give consumers the benefits of a competitive market. This legislation represents a positive step forward and deserves widespread support."

The next sentence leaped out at me: "Unfortunately, certain special interest groups are actively seeking exceptions from deregulation for certain categories of natural gas."

I was thinking, "You bet they are, Mr. Chairman, just as your company had obtained language in the legislation to ensure that it would be able to break its contracts and reap windfall profits." This letter was exactly what I would have expected Texaco management to tell their shareholders.

McKinley finished by urging the shareholders to write their senators and representatives to "enlist their support for total decontrol of *all* natural gas *without* exception." It included a postage-paid return card for use if the reader desired "additional information regarding identification of your senator and representative."

I sent copies of the letter with an "FYI" note to Foster and the rest of the First Four, and then briefed Bob Steder.

CHAPTER FORTY-NINE

"HE'LL JUST INSERT THE LANGUAGE"

SEPTEMBER 17, 9:20 A.M. -- MIKE BOLAND, Jim Broyhill's man and the minority staff counsel to Phil Sharp's subcommittee, was on the phone. "Ed," he began, "Mr. Broyhill asked me to let you know that Ralph Hall is going to add language to the staff draft that would allow deregulated pricing for gas brought up by what are called enhanced recovery methods."

Damn! Bill Foster was right, except they're trying for it first in the House. I thanked Boland for the heads-up, explained that I knew what the term meant, and asked if he knew whether Texaco was trying to put the same language into the Senate bill. He said he had no idea.

Foster answered my phone call with, "I just heard about it, Ed, from Dingell's staff. So when and where do you want the crew to meet?"

My first thought was to hold the meeting at PPG; then I reconsidered. "This should be a full coalition meeting, don't you think?"

"It'd be good to get their thinking as well," Foster agreed. "So set it up with King and Rosemary, and let me know when and where. I'll see what information I can bring to the meeting."

As I put down the phone, Tena came in and said Mary Jo Zacchero was holding on another line. I picked up the phone and began with, "Let me guess, M.J.; you're calling to tell me about Ralph Hall putting enhanced recovery language into your staff draft, right?"

There was the slightest of pauses, and Zacchero said, "News travels fast. How'd you find out?"

"Mike Boland just called, at Broyhill's request."

"So are you surprised?"

"I would've been, but Bill Foster told us a month ago that he anticipated just this sort of approach, although he figured it might come up first in the Senate. He's gotten approval for a Senate floor colloquy between McClure and Johnston to spell out that enhanced recovery gas was meant to be treated the same as old gas in the bill." Then I added, "But that's on the Senate floor. We really hadn't figured that Annett and John Camp would push it in the Sharp subcommittee. Looks like we should've."

"I agree. So what do you guys want to do about it?"

"I just got off the phone with Foster and was about to set up a meeting of the two coalitions, all ten of us, for tomorrow, hopefully at Freeport McMoRan, Russell King's company. They're upstairs in our building." I thought about asking M.J. to the meeting, but realized that might put her in a compromising position. "How about if I get back to you immediately after we meet, probably either late tomorrow morning or in the afternoon?"

"Okay, but just don't wait too long."

"How soon do you think Hall's gonna move on this?"

"He's not likely to wait for another markup session. No, instead, I'd expect him to have minority staff just insert the language into the staff draft, leaving it up to you guys to knock it out."

"Charming," I replied. "Here we go again. It's Senate Energy redux, in a sense."

"That it is. So call me ASAP, okay?"

"You got it. And thanks for the call, M.J."

I decided to walk upstairs and see King personally. He was at his desk, and after I explained the situation, he immediately agreed to a meeting in his conference room tomorrow at 1 p.m., figuring that holding off until then gave us a better chance to have all the players there. He would call the rest of the Second Six, and I would alert Cole, Dale and Ferguson as well as Foster and Sara Schotland.

CHAPTER FIFTY

"THE TOUGH PART IS NOT KNOWING THE IMPACT"

SEPTEMBER 18, 1 P.M. -- THE FULL complement of Washington reps and outside lawyers were in the room. Schotland sat beside me, with Foster at one end of the conference table and King at the other, O'Brien at his side.

I began by briefing everyone on yesterday's phone calls from Boland and Zacchero. Foster then said he had met yesterday afternoon with Boland and was told the language to be added to the staff draft would be a new section of the bill, titled "Production of New Enhancement Natural Gas." There would also be clarifying language written for the committee report.

(A committee report, sometimes called legislative history, generally accompanies any legislation that is approved by a full committee, and sometimes a subcommittee as well. Its main function is to clarify the intent of the committee or subcommittee in approving the bill. Similarly, when Senate-House conferees have agreed on legislation, they issue a conference report. That report is basically the marching orders for the federal department or agency tasked with administering and/or overseeing that legislation once it

becomes law. It has also often been a focus of legal challenges to the law it accompanies.)

"So, did you get any specifics from Boland as to what's being put into the staff draft?" asked O'Brien.

"Other than the title of the new section, nothing yet," said Foster. "From our group's perspective, I'm pretty sure we'll get it as soon as it's written, from Boland and Zacchero. Who has other contacts they can tap?"

Several hands were raised. "Good," I offered. "Let's be sure we compare notes on that, like tomorrow?" I looked at King and O'Brien as I said this; both nodded agreement.

"As you know," Foster added, "it's likely Texaco will try to put the exact same language into the Senate bill on the floor. That's assuming they succeed in getting it into Sharp's staff draft, and I have some information on that."

I was wondering why Foster hadn't briefed me in advance on his actions since yesterday's phone call. "Sounds as if you've been a busy man," I said, looking straight at Bill. If he was flustered at all, it didn't show.

"Had to do a bit of scrambling, and got this last bit of info late this morning. It appears that Mr. Hall huddled with Chairman Sharp, and that Mr. Shelby of Alabama was also in the meeting. Apparently, they persuaded the subcommittee chairman that 'the other side', as they called it, and I'd say they meant Texaco, deserved at least some recourse, after, as they put it, the 'lightning speed' with which Walgren's amendment was brought up and voted on."

I shook my head slightly, thinking that this was the flip side of the good work Doug Walgren and Mary Jo had done for us.

Cole spoke next. "So it appears that our first job is to find out just when that staff draft will be considered in Sharp's subcommittee, and then to try to knock the language out of it."

Cole's natural vocal inflection made his comment sound like a question, and a member of the Second Six, an outside attorney from Borden, attending one of our meetings for the first time, said, "Hold it a minute. How much gas are we talking about? I mean, is it a huge amount, or are we just nibbling at the margins here?"

Foster answered. "We obviously don't know that yet. As the rest of the folks here know from when I explained how enhanced recovery works, it could be a fairly small amount. Or it could be a whole lot of gas. I doubt that Texaco would bother making this push if they didn't think it was worthwhile."

Schotland joined the discussion. "I agree with Bill, and there's also the likelihood that Texaco will try to write the language in a way that will give the broadest possible interpretation of what's included in enhanced recovery gas."

"So what's our first step?" asked Cole.

Foster looked over at Schotland, then answered. "I'd say you guys get us all the specifics you can about the language, ASAP, and then let the attorneys see what they can develop and get that back to each of you, okay?"

Cole, I and a few others nodded; no one disagreed, and the meeting ended. I went downstairs to phone Zacchero.

* * *

SEPTEMBER 25, 1:30 P.M. -- It had taken a week, but we finally had Texaco's language. It was Sara Schotland who first got it over to me, and it closely fit the rationale Bill Foster had explained to us back in June. Stripped of the legalese, the provision basically held that natural gas derived through tertiary recovery, infill drilling or any other method of enhanced recovery was, in fact, newly found gas and thus should not be included in the definition of "old gas," i.e., gas produced before 1977.

Therefore, went the rationale, this gas clearly should be decontrolled in price.

I immediately phoned Bob Steder and read him the language, then asked, "Any idea at all of how much gas this would involve for us?"

"No idea at all," came the reply. "We'd have to know how much Texaco can get through enhanced recovery. But hell, Ed, can't you guys knock this language out of the bill? I mean, you've won a helluva lot bigger battles than this in this war."

I swallowed, then had to explain to Steder the situation that led Sharp to accept Ralph Hall's proposed language in the staff draft. Essentially, I told Steder, it was payback for Sharp having allowed Walgren to move his amendment -- the one that helped us -- to the head of the list in markup.

"So it's a case of 'be careful what you ask for,' right?"

"You could definitely say that, yes. But Bob, we'll do everything we can to get this out of the bill. Though, to be frank, it doesn't look easy. I'll start by checking with Mary Jo Zacchero. And I fully expect Sara Schotland and her team to be involved, as well as the lawyers at Patton Boggs. The tough part, though, is not knowing the specific impact on us if this thing goes through."

"So we both have a problem," Steder concluded.

CHAPTER FIFTY-ONE

"DON'T HOLD YOUR BREATH"

OCTOBER 21, 2 P.M. -- THE FULL group, with Foster and Schotland, were gathered at Kaiser's Washington office. While waiting for action in the Sharp subcommittee -- and now openly hoping the bill would continue to languish there -- we had renewed our Senate contacts with key members. We knew we had Senators McClure, Johnston and Ford firmly on our side, and decided to focus our efforts on Majority Leader Howard Baker plus ten members of the Energy Committee: Senators Bradley, Bumpers, Cochran, Domenici, Hatfield, Melcher, Nickles, Nunn, Stevens and Wallop. And at Foster's suggestion, we added Russell Long to the list, with plans to have Bennett Johnston speak with him. Cole, who had originally volunteered to see Long, agreed fully with this strategy.

As a result of our visits, we learned two key things. First, and surprisingly, not one of the senators we spoke with said he had changed his opinion since the May 5 vote.

"I'd have expected at least two or three to have been swayed the other way in five months," I said.

Cole responded with, "Don't lose sight of the fact that despite the publicity our particular battle has generated, it's still just one small part of a huge and extremely complex bill. These guys have all sorts of issues they're being pressed to support or oppose."

That made sense, of course. But it was what we learned next that may have put things even more clearly.

"I spoke with Senator Baker's office this morning," reported Foster. "He said we shouldn't hold our breath expecting this bill to come to the floor this year."

My brows were halfway up my forehead as I asked Foster, "Were those their exact words, or are you interpreting what was said."

"Ed, I was a bit surprised too, but that's exactly what I was told. That, plus there's a really crowded calendar for floor action through at least November, and these guys would like to leave for Christmas by December 20 at the latest."

Foster's report may have helped explain why the senators we had seen said they hadn't changed their opinion. If they knew, or even suspected, that the decontrol bill was done for this year, they likely wouldn't have spent much time at all worrying about it. So we might also put contacting Senator Long on the back burner.

And that also meant that for now, at least, we could focus all our efforts on Phil Sharp's House subcommittee. The first thing on my "to do" list would be to check in with Mary Jo Zacchero. Then I would contact Bob Steder, send an update memo to PPG management, and get Sara Schotland's view of Texaco's latest move.

CHAPTER FIFTY-TWO

"WE CAN SIT DOWN TOGETHER"

OCTOBER 22, 9:20 A.M. -- I HAD just gotten off the phone with Zacchero, who had suggested an approach. "I really doubt that we can knock Mr. Hall's language out of the staff draft at this point, but just in case, why don't you prepare alternative language, as possible amendments to the Texaco language, and Doug will look at what you've got. Then we can sit down together -- probably you and your attorneys -- and discuss the situation."

"Sounds like a plan to me, M.J. But let me ask you, do you see the subcommittee completing the markup anytime soon?"

"Frankly, no, I don't, Ed. But you want to cover all the bases, right?"

"Absolutely. I'll get back to you soon as we have something to discuss."

* * *

NOVEMBER 4, 9:05 A.M. -- Sara Schotland had just sent over a memo to both me and PPG general counsel Dick Packard. Her approach was different in that it still focused on the Senate instead of the House.

She had reasoned that with House action seemingly stalled but with the minority staff having added their enhanced recovery provision to the staff draft, Texaco might try to insert similar language in the Senate bill. They obviously felt that adding their amendment in the Senate might be easier once the House subcommittee had accepted it. But that had been the subcommittee staff's decision, and not the members'; there had been no vote on the matter, making it much the same approach as Senator Johnston had orchestrated for us many months ago.

Basically, Schotland's wording comported with the approach Foster had used in crafting his floor colloquy. The Cleary Gottleib wording was aimed at clarifying that any enhanced recovery provisions in the bill would apply to natural gas sold "for resale," thus exempting gas sold to the companies in our group.

That approach, if successfully inserted, would work in both the House and Senate versions of the legislation. The proposed amendment would add language stating that, "Notwithstanding any other provision of this Act, the provisions of Subtitle A respecting the maximum lawful price shall not apply to the first sale of new enhancement natural gas."

That seemed pretty clean and clear to me. Schotland also appended some conforming language for the draft legislative history. I phoned her with my thanks and asked if she had heard back from Dick Packard on it.

"Not yet, but I called Dick just before sending this to him and asked that he get back to me this morning if possible."

"Well, how about if we set up a conference call among the three of us after he reads it. Assuming he agrees with me that the approach and the language look good, I'd like to bring Mary Jo Zacchero into the loop."

"Why?"

"Because when I spoke with her last week, she said there was still a chance, however small, that Texaco's amendment could be knocked out of the subcommittee staff draft. At the least, she offered to look over whatever fix we come up with. I'd like to work on both houses of Congress on this, if you and Dick Packard agree."

"What's Zacchero's take on the future of the House bill?"

"I asked her the same question, and she said she doesn't see markup on the bill ending anytime soon. I didn't ask if that meant before the end of this year."

"I guess my view is, why shoot that bullet, in the House, if the bill's not going anywhere?"

"That's a valid question," I admitted. "But look, Mary Jo and Doug Walgren have been by far our best supporters on this thing in the House. I just think we owe it to her to keep her in the loop."

"Okay, just so long as we're not painting ourselves into a corner, Ed."

"Well, let's have that three-way discussion, and we'll go from there."

Sara agreed.

* * *

NOVEMBER 4, 11:25 A. M. – Schotland was back on the line, and she had set up the conference call with Dick Packard.

I began the discussion with, "Dick, I assume you've read Sara's proposed amending language, right?"

"Yes."

I figured Sara must have gotten Packard's approval for the wording before setting up the conference call. "And it looks good to you?" I asked.

"I have no problem with it, but Sara tells me you think we should try to put it into both the Senate and House versions of the bill."

"I do, Dick, even though it seems there's a pretty good chance neither house of Congress will complete action on the legislation this year. And frankly, we may not be able to get this language into the House bill."

Packard seemed surprised at the likelihood of no further legislative action this year.

"That's the reading I get from Doug Walgren's legislative aide for energy issues, and she's been spot on so far about Chairman Sharp's subcommittee. And you saw the line in Sara's memo that it seems unlikely the bill will reach the Senate floor this year either."

"That's true," Schotland added.

"Well, for the record," I said, "I agree that Sara's proposed language works well, and I'd like to try to put it into the Senate version and at least *try* to get it into the House bill as well. It'd be a pre-emptive strike in the Senate and a defensive move in the House. As Sara points out, Texaco may make their move in the Senate fairly quickly, now that they have their language in the House committee staff draft."

"Do you think the other members of the coalition will agree with that approach?"

"That's a good question, Dick. I'd have to sound them out first, of course."

"Okay. Do that. And assuming there's agreement, who will you work with in the Senate on this?"

I paused for a moment, knowing that other law firms would likely become involved, and that Patton Boggs definitely would. "I'd include Bill Foster, our key man from Patton Boggs, in the meeting to review the language. Foster's been our point man with Bennett Johnston, who as you know is ranking minority on the Senate Energy Committee. That means Johnston will be a key floor manager of the bill when and if it reaches the Senate floor."

Packard had one more question: "And you'll include Sara in your meeting to review the language, right?"

"Of course. She'll be the one who explains the wording."

"Then, Sara, if it's okay with you, I'd say let's go ahead and give this thing a shot ... in both houses."

Schotland, who had been mostly quiet during the discussion, said, "Assuming this thing is a 'go' with the coalition, I'll join Ed in talking with Doug Walgren's aide, and we'll look at the Senate as soon as we see if we can get the amendment into the House bill."

"Good. Just keep me posted."

CHAPTER FIFTY-THREE

"THE HEAVY LIFTING..."

NOVEMBER 12, 1 P.M. -- WE WERE in Mary Jo Zacchero's office. Schotland had explained her proposed amending language at a meeting of the full 10-company coalition on November 6, and while two of the lawyers had wanted a day to noodle over the wording, things had gone surprising smoothly. Changes to one or two words, or a comma here and there, but nothing that in any way altered the intent and approach of Sara's proposal.

Mary Jo looked over the wording and nodded. "Short and sweet. Looks good to me. But that refers to the language. The heavy lifting will be in getting Sharp and his staff to agree to your approach. Don't forget, it carves out an exemption from the enhanced recovery language that Mr. Hall had the staff insert for Texaco."

"Well," I began, "it clearly wouldn't make sense for me to try to talk to Mike Boland or any other minority staffer on this, M.J. So what would you suggest?"

Zacchero chuckled and said, "That's a nice way of asking me if I'll carry the ball for you guys, right?"

I smiled, "Something like that."

EDWARD L. JAFFEE

"Let me talk to Doug about it. If he has no objections, I'll give it a shot. But again, I really don't see the subcommittee finishing this thing this year. In fact, I'm beginning to doubt if Mr. Sharp will even reconvene the markup before at least January. There are several other bills scheduled for subcommittee action this year."

"So," asked Schotland, "assuming you're right and that nothing more gets done this year, do you agree it's still a good idea to try to get this amendment into the bill next year?"

"As I said, let's first see what Mr. Walgren thinks. If he agrees with you folks, then yes, we'll try for it, whenever we get word that the subcommittee's getting back to the bill."

"That's all we can ask in the House," I said, and then explained that we would try the same approach in the Senate, having Bill Foster work through Senator Johnston and the Energy Committee staff.

"That's *their* business," Zacchero replied. "I'm assuming you want to get the language into the Senate bill before Texaco tries to get their amendment accepted over there, right?"

Both Sara and I nodded.

CHAPTER FIFTY-FOUR

"YOU GUYS FIRM ...?"

FEBRUARY 5, 1984, 9:34 A.M. – THE TIMING of the Sharp subcommittee markup surprised us. Mary Jo Zacchero phoned me to say that chairman Sharp had scheduled the action for one week from today. I responded by asking her if Mr. Walgren was ready to go back to bat for us in this round.

"The answer is 'yes,' but why don't you, Bob Cole and Bill Foster drop by here this afternoon if you can make it, and let's discuss tactics."

"You got it."

* * *

FEBRUARY 5, 1:30 P.M. -- Cole, Foster, Zacchero and I were in chairs in Mr. Walgren's office while he was on the House floor. "You guys are asking Mr. Walgren to take on both chairman Sharp and ranking member Hall on this thing. Just wanted to be sure you realize what he has to do here."

"We do realize that, M.J., and believe me, we do appreciate it."

Before I could add anything more, Bill Foster spoke up. "Mr. Walgren knows, of course, that Mr. Sharp has to be considering the future of this bill in the full committee and that Sharp certainly wants to do all he can to gain Chairman Dingell's support. Wouldn't you agree?"

"You're thinking ahead, Bill ... and you're right, of course."

I jumped in: "So, since Doug's vote is crucial to Mr. Sharp at this stage, and since you told us earlier that Doug feels the full committee vote might be extremely close as well ..."

Zacchero finished my sentence, "Then all Doug has to do is remind Sharp of his position. Is that what you're saying?"

"Pretty much," I replied.

"I'll tell him that's what you guys said."

"Well," Cole added, "however you think is best."

"I'm just pulling your chain, guys. Don't worry, Doug knows how to work with Chairman Sharp. And I'll be involved as well, with the committee staff. You guys firm on the language you showed me earlier?"

Foster said, "Yes, we are," and Cole and I nodded.

"Then get out of here and let me get to work."

CHAPTER FIFTY-FIVE

"DO YOU THINK TEXACO WILL TRY AGAIN?"

FEBRUARY 12, 10 A.M. -- THE FIRST Four and Foster, plus Rosemary O'Brien and Russell King were seated toward the back in the Fossil and Synthetic Fuels Subcommittee hearing room in the Rayburn House Office Building. George White sat a few rows farther forward. Sara Schotland had opted not to attend, as was her usual approach. It seemed that Mary Jo Zacchero and Doug Walgren had worked their magic yet again; Zacchero had told me things looked solid for us to add our amendment to the Texaco language.

Chairman Sharp gaveled the session to order. With perfect aplomb and a dry wit, he began: "So as we were saying when we last met on this bill just the other day … ." The room erupted in laughter, including Don Annett of Texaco, who sat alone closer to the front.

Sharp had the chief counsel to the subcommittee explain the changes that were in the staff draft. When that was done, the committee clerk proceeded to read through each section, and votes were cast to accept or reject the changes.

When the clerk finally reached our section of the bill, our group held its collective breath. The clerk intoned the words, "Notwithstanding any other provisions of this Act, the provisions of Subtitle A with respect to the maximum lawful price shall not apply to the first sale of new enhancement natural gas."

Annett was sitting bolt upright. Could he conceivably have not seen our language? Had he been focused solely on the language he had gotten into the staff draft? No, I said to myself, no chance of that.

The chairman called for the yeas and nays on our amendment, and Sara Schotland's wording was approved, by a 14-4 vote. The margin surprised all of us.

Our group did our best to keep a collective poker face, while Annett was out of his seat quickly and quietly, heading for the door.

"Uh oh," I said to Bob Cole on my right, "looks like Mary Jo's about to get another earful."

This time the seven of us stayed until the clerk had read through all the changes to the staff draft, with votes on each one. At that point, Chairman Sharp called for a vote on accepting the staff draft as a substitute for the original bill. That vote carried by a 12-6 margin, a virtual assurance that the revised bill would also pass.

The final vote on the subcommittee bill was 10-8, a bit closer than I had expected, but definitely good enough for us. As the subcommittee members rose to leave, Doug Walgren looked over at our group and offered a slight nod.

While the others headed back to their offices, I found a pay phone and relayed the news to Sara, then headed over to thank Mary Jo yet again for all she had done.

Mr. Walgren had beaten me back to his office and was talking with M.J. I stood back until he motioned me over.

Shaking my head and grinning as I walked up, I extended my right hand. "Congressman, we can't thank you enough for all you've done ... well, you and Mary Jo."

"No problem, it was the right thing to do. Now I have some other things to tend to," he added, leaving me with M.J.

"Did Don Annett land on you again?" I asked.

"No, didn't see him. So, do you think Texaco will try again in full committee?"

"Funny, I was going to ask you the same thing."

"Well, let me know what your group thinks, and I'll keep my eyes open. But frankly, Ed, I don't know how many more shots they'll take. I mean, they must realize that they're not going to turn this thing around with Mr. Dingell. He owes them no favors, so why would he arbitrarily want to change what Mr. Sharp's subcommittee did, on a provision as minor to Dingell as this one?"

"Do you feel confident in that?" I asked.

"I do, and for the reason we've discussed before. Both Chairman Sharp and Chairman Dingell realize they need Doug's vote to get this bill through full committee."

"I think it's time for me to send another report to corporate headquarters, emphasizing the key role you guys have played."

CHAPTER FIFTY-SIX

"HEADING INTO THE NINTH INNING"

APRIL 16, 12:30 P.M. --THE FIRST Four and Bill Foster were meeting over lunch. After a belated celebratory toast, we got down to business. I had heard nothing further from Walgren's office since the February 12 subcommittee action. Bill Foster had gotten an advance look at the subcommittee report and found nothing in it that might counteract our win. "Looks as if Texaco may be either giving up on the enhanced recovery language, or getting ready to try to delete our 'not for resale' language in full committee. And, of course, there's still the Senate floor vote to worry about. We'd better stay on our toes in both houses."

Nothing more had happened on the legislation in the Senate. Foster had shown our proposed amendment to Senator Johnston, who said it looked good but opted to hold off on pushing for it until the Senate leadership signaled its intent to bring the bill up on the floor.

As we were finishing our meal, a waiter came up to Foster, saying he had a phone call. Bill excused himself as the rest of us chatted about other matters in our lives. Things seemed calm for now.

But then Foster returned, with major news. Bill O'Hara had just heard from Dave Finnegan, a key aide to John Dingell, that the full

House Energy and Commerce Committee had scheduled markup on the bill, H.R. 1760, for April 22.

"That gives us six days to make sure our ducks are still in a row, and to make sure Texaco doesn't get a reversal of our win in the subcommittee," said Ferguson.

"No rest for the weary," echoed Cole.

* * *

APRIL 16, 2 P.M. -- We had gone from lunch to Cole's office. Foster called back to Patton Boggs to ask O'Hara if he knew whether Dingell had heard from Texaco. The answer was "yes," but not for the past three weeks, and then only about the enhanced recovery language.

That meant the coalition most likely needed first to contact Dingell's man Dave Finnegan -- well, after I checked back with Zacchero -- to see if we could get a reading on just how solid our "not for resale" language was, in Chairman Dingell's eyes. And we needed, once more, to at least contact the four key political bloc members we had chosen, and maybe to contact many more on the 42-person committee.

As Foster pointed out, for those who had supported us on the issue in subcommittee, our calls and/or visits would be just to touch base and reaffirm their support. We would ignore those we knew would not support us, making the workload more manageable.

The one wild card was Billy Tauzin. Cole thought we should see him. "If we were able to get Tauzin's vote, that might send a signal to Texaco that the game is over, and dissuade them from trying to delete our 'for resale' language on the Senate floor as well."

"It's worth a shot," opined Foster. "Can you try him, Bob?"

"I'll try," Cole answered. "Now, let's go back over our choices as leaders of the four blocs. As I recall it, we had Paul Rogers for the liberal Democrats, Walgren for the moderate Dems, Corcoran for the moderate Republicans and Jim Broyhill for the conservative Repubs, right?"

"Right," I answered, "but Corcoran was involved in reviving the subcommittee markup when Texaco's enhanced recovery fix was first added, and I'm wondering whether he's still the guy we should use as leverage."

"Good point," Cole admitted. "So who do you see as our man?"

"If you remember," I said, "Don Ritter was our second choice. And he did volunteer that he's close with Walgren."

"Sounds reasonable to me," said Foster. Nobody disagreed.

"So we have another 'first four,' as it were," added Lew Dale. "Who are some of the others we'll need to hit this week?"

Cole pulled out a Congressional Staff Directory, an indispensible resource for every Washington representative, in that it listed all the members of both houses of Congress plus their key aides, and their committee and subcommittee assignments, as well as the composition of each committee and subcommittee and the staffers for all of those groups. Office addresses and phone numbers were also included.

Despite the hope that our four key members of the committee would agree to try to sway at least some of the other congressmen in their blocs, we realized we needed to consider having to contact the majority of committee members. We spent the next hour poring over the roster of the Energy and Commerce Committee. Seeing Mr. Dingell, or at least Finnegan, was a given. Just who could manage to see "Mr. Chairman" might be another matter, though Cole was closest with him.

We looked at each of the four blocs, and assessed -- without great certainty but based on their voting records -- whom to put in each group. We started with the liberal Democrats, a group that included Reps. Paul Rogers, Henry Waxman, Tim Wirth, Ed Markey, Al Gore, Dick Ottinger of New York, Jim Florio of New Jersey, Barbara Mikulski of Maryland, Cardiss Collins of Illinois, Jim Scheuer of New York, and Ron Wyden of Oregon.

Our moderate Democratic group included Dingell, Walgren, Sharp, Al Swift of Washington, Tom Luken of Ohio, Dowdy, Bill Richardson of New Mexico, Jim Oberstar of Minnesota and Richard Shelby of Alabama, though Bill Foster noted that Shelby was really a conservative Democrat (and, in fact, Shelby later switched parties). We also listed Billy Tauzin in this group. We would not bother trying to see Mickey Leland of Texas or Oklahoma's Mike Synar.

Our estimate of the moderate-to-conservative Republican group included Don Ritter, Tom Corcoran, Jim Slattery of Kansas and Matt Rinaldo of New Jersey.

And the conservative Republicans we listed included Broyhill, Madigan, Oxley, Carlos Moorhead, Jim Bates and Bill Dannemeyer of California, Norm Lent of New York, Dan Coats of Indiana, Bob Whittaker of Kansas, Howard Nielsen of Utah and Tom Bliley of Virginia. We would ignore Ralph Hall, John Bryant, Bob Eckhardt and Jack Fields, all from Texas, as being virtually certain to support Texaco in whatever move they might decide to make.

For the record, that made 23 Democrats and 19 Republicans, but we knew that party lines might matter less than usual in how members voted on this complex legislation. We had plans to contact 36 of the 42 members or their key aides.

For the members we had seen before, our assignments remained the same. For those on the full committee who had not been on our list, we would first try to leverage the leaders of the four political blocs, but also work with the Washington reps from the Second Six to see as many of these people as we could. We figured that George White would have the lead with Mr. Rogers, Bill Simpson would of course be our point man with Mr. Dowdy, Rosemary O'Brien would be key in seeing Messrs. Slattery, Whittaker, Oberstar, Collins, and again with my help, Madigan. All of those last five members were from the breadbasket of the country and represented districts that were heavy users of CF Industries' fertilizer products.

So the game was on, once again. What we did not know was that we were going into the ninth inning.

CHAPTER FIFTY-SEVEN

"TIME TO GET TOMMY BOGGS IN HARNESS"

APRIL 17, 10 A.M. -- OUR COMBINED groups had met and agreed on our assignments. Bob Cole and I were once again in Doug Walgren's office with the congressman and Mary Jo Zacchero.

Mary Jo began the conversation, advising that, "This vote still looks just as close as we've thought all along. So, what's your plan of attack?"

"Beyond asking for my help," Walgren added.

"We plan to follow your earlier advice, and break up the full committee along political blocs as much as possible ... liberal Democrats, moderate-to-conservative Democrats, moderate Republicans and conservative Republicans." Mary Jo mentioned the four members we had chosen to reach first in the Sharp subcommittee, and I added that, "we've decided to switch from Mr. Corcoran to Don Ritter for the moderate Republicans."

"Well, that may be a good choice," said Walgren.

Cole chimed in with, "After that, we figure we need to contact thirty-two other members or their offices. We don't see a high percentage in trying for the members from Texas or Oklahoma."

I added, "And, of course, there's Chairman Dingell. Patton Boggs will be helping us there, and Bob here also knows Mr. Dingell, while I've worked with Dave Finnegan on environmental issues."

"That's all well and good," countered Walgren, "but have you thought about also using Phil Sharp as leverage with Dingell?"

Cole looked at me, and I replied, "Congressman, we were hoping you could help us on that one, by talking with Mr. Sharp and letting him get the message that your vote is still important, if not key, to getting the bill through full committee."

Walgren nodded and said, "I can try that, meeting again with Sharp, but you folks still need to make your pitch to Sharp as well. Just be sure to coordinate with Mary Jo to make sure we're giving the same message."

We thanked Walgren and walked out into the hall. "So, who's our best person or persons to see Sharp?" I wondered aloud.

Cole thought for a moment, then suggested we first use Tommy Boggs, then follow up with a small group visit if we could swing it.

"And who do you see making up that small group?" I asked.

"First, I'd suggest Rosemary O'Brien. Don't forget, Indiana is heavily agricultural. We should include Foster, plus you and Russell King as key people in the two coalitions."

"What about you?" I asked.

"I don't think we need to overcrowd the meeting, if Sharp's willing to meet."

I said, "Okay, we'll tell the others at our next meeting, which better be pretty quick. Now, what about Dingell? I'm thinking this is the time for us to push Foster into getting Tommy Boggs into play, to contact Dingell and Billy Tauzin. I figure that since Tommy's roots are in Louisiana as well as Washington, he might be in a good position to see Billy."

"Ed, that's playing hardball. I mean, Patton Boggs is making a bundle in fees from the First Four, and Tauzin might see the obvious conflict of interest here."

"Conflict? Hell, Bob, Foster's been in this thing up to his neck from the start. And you don't think John Camp's been involved, however quietly?"

It was Cole's turn to pause. Then, "Yeah, I guess you're right, and we're certainly down to the short strokes. Plus, Tommy figures to have a better shot at getting Dingell than I would. So, you're gonna call Foster, right?"

"Soon as I get back to the office. Then we'll set up the full group meeting for tomorrow at my place. That should give Foster time to talk with Tommy and give us a report."

* * *

APRIL 17, 11:30 A.M. – Foster's initial response to my suggestion about bringing Tommy Boggs into the picture was to be hesitant. "I don't know, Ed. Can't we pull this off without using Tommy?"

I thought back to our first meeting with Patton Boggs, when they agreed to represent us. "It's your show, Bill," Boggs had said to Foster. But he had said something else as well.

"Bill," I began, "You've done a hell of a job for us right from the start. There's no doubt about that, and we all know it. But remember that at our first meeting with you guys, Tommy did say he'll be involved as necessary. Next week will be the key vote in the House committee, and Cole and I agree it's time to get Tommy in harness for the heavy pulling, with Sharp and Dingell and also with Tauzin."

"Tauzin? You still want to go for the jugular?"

"He's a member of the full committee. We're covering almost everyone on the committee, so why not include him?"

"You realize, of course, that he'll alert Texaco as soon as we see him."

"Maybe so, maybe not. And we could always hold off on seeing him until last. Word will get around in any case, Bill, so why not try for Tauzin along with the others?"

"I guess it's worth a shot. And yes, Tommy did volunteer to make some contacts if we need him. I'll talk to him about it."

"It would help if you can do that today. We'd like to get the full group together here at PPG tomorrow morning at 9:30, or at least as many as can make it, and you could give us your report then, Bill. We only have a few days to make all these contacts."

"I'll see you tomorrow."

CHAPTER FIFTY-EIGHT

"INFILL DRILLING"

APRIL 18, 9:30 A.M. -- "FOUR DAYS, people, that's all we have until the full committee markup and vote. We need to work fast," I emphasized.

Foster spoke up. "I think I can offer something that'll make our job a bit easier. I spoke with Tommy Boggs yesterday afternoon, and he phoned Mr. Dingell. The report is that Dingell is really anxious to get this bill out of committee and over to the Rules Committee. He's excellent at counting votes in his committee, and he knows Doug Walgren's vote is pivotal to him. So, Ed, we've gotten Walgren to go to bat for us before. Will he do it again?"

I smiled at the way Foster had left out my phone call to him yesterday, and had also put the ball back into my court. But that was fine; Bill had gotten Tommy to make the key phone call. Contacting Tauzin could wait, but what about Sharp?

"First, that's great news about Tommy," I said. "Well done. And as for Walgren, he agreed yesterday to help us again, but he emphasized that we need to see Dingell and Sharp as well. Looks like Dingell's taken care of." Then, turning to Cole, I added, "Bob has some ideas about a small group meeting with Sharp, if you all agree."

Cole reviewed his plan that O'Brien, Foster, King and I try to get a meeting with Mr. Sharp. O'Brien just nodded, but Russell King, usually an eager and agreeable type, surprised me by snapping at Cole and me, "It would've been nice if you guys had alerted me yesterday to your plan."

Surprised at King's tone, I said, "Sorry, Russell. You're right, and I forgot to call."

At that moment, the sound of a jackhammer invaded the room. Somewhere below us, an office was being renovated. "What was *that*!?" Lew Dale asked.

"Infill drilling," deadpanned Ferguson. It broke the tension.

King was chuckling. "Okay, so who's gonna make the phone call to Sharp's office?"

I looked at Foster and asked, "Bill, can you handle that?"

"I'll try, soon as this meeting is over. And Tommy has a phone call into him as well."

With that, we went though the full committee roster, asking members of the Second Six, including George White, to take the lead where it was appropriate. Time was short, the stakes were high, and nobody disagreed. We had 96 hours to sink or swim in the House Energy and Commerce Committee.

CHAPTER FIFTY-NINE

CHAIRMAN DINGELL CALLS FOR THE YEAS AND NAYS

APRIL 22, 9:55 A.M. – THE WHOLE team, all ten companies, our outside counsel (including Sara Schotland this time), plus Foster were gathered in the hall outside the Energy and Commerce Committee hearing room on the first floor of the Rayburn House Office Building.

We had made all of our visits and/or calls, and Boggs and Foster had set up the meeting with Phil Sharp, but the subcommittee chairman had given no assurances that he would go to bat for us with Chairman Dingell. Knowing that Boggs had contacted Mr. Dingell, we had gently suggested that Sharp check again with the full committee chairman about protecting our position. But Sharp was still reluctant, saying only, "There are many, many issues at stake in this legislation. Yours is just one of those issues, and I'm not going to make a big deal out of it at this time."

"At this time." Those works stuck with me. Had Doug Walgren been unsuccessful in reinforcing his position with Sharp? If that wasn't the case, what kind of game was Sharp playing?

DODGING THE BULLET

I had gone back to Zacchero, who told me Doug had indeed met again with Sharp, but also reaffirmed that Sharp was being cagey. She had said she would talk with senior subcommittee staff to urge them to push the point, but that staff was not likely to even consider questioning their boss.

So there was nothing to do but wait out the vote. The old anxieties from the Senate Energy Committee vote poured over me as we entered the hearing room. But again, Bill Foster seemed totally placid.

The committee clerk began by reading the title and brief purpose of the bill and then proceeded to read each section. Mr. Sharp or another member would routinely ask that the section be considered as read and open for amendment. There were a variety of those offered throughout the process. The committee broke for lunch at 12:15 p.m. and returned at 1:30, and the markup dragged on.

Chairman Dingell, as was his wont, was making sure every legislative rule of order was being observed. It slowed the process, and at 3 p.m., the chairman noted the time and advised the members that it was his intent to "stay here today until we finish this bill." Several people slipped out of the room, probably to make phone calls rearranging their evening plans.

By 7:10 p.m., the markup was finally approaching our section. There had been no adjournment for dinner, and none of us seemed to notice any hunger pangs.

And finally, at 7:25 p.m., the clerk read our section. *No amendments were offered!* Texaco had not even tried to delete our "for resale" language, or our fix to the enhanced recovery language, from the bill. They had either not approached Mr. Hall or Billy Tauzin to carry their amendment or those two members had declined to do so, and apparently they had also doped out that they lacked the votes.

All that remained was the final vote to report the bill. That and the committee report language.

When the vote came, at 9:24 p.m., we knew we were safe either way, for now. But we also knew now that it would be best for us if the bill passed the full committee. Otherwise, there was always the possibility, however unlikely, that next year, with a new start on a new bill, we might lose. And of course, there was also the possibility that we might have to start over with Patton Boggs, a costly proposition for the First Four, and perhaps an idea not so appealing to our law firm either. Given the media coverage, they wanted a win, now, almost as much as we needed it.

Chairman Dingell called for the yeas and nays, and the clerk intoned the names of the committee members, with the chairman voting last.

Doug Walgren had nailed the count yet again, as had Phil Sharp. The bill carried by a single vote, 21-20, with one member absent and with Walgren, Sharp and Dingell all voting "yes." And there was one other member whose vote was key: Mr. Tauzin of Louisiana voted to pass the bill, most likely because he supported the broader aim of decontrolling prices.

* * *

APRIL 22, 9:55 P.M. -- When it was over, I asked Foster about Billy Tauzin. "I knew Texaco hadn't gotten his support," he said.

"And you said nothing to me about it. What did Tauzin say when Tommy talked with him?"

"All Tommy told me was that Billy said, 'It was the right thing to do.'"

It was the same answer many members give when asked to explain their vote. The same answer Doug Walgren had given me earlier.

Meanwhile, the more important factor was Walgren's support for the bill. As Mary Jo told me later, Sharp had been deliberately holding his cards close to the vest, making deals with a number of members for their support. And, M. J. reported, it had all come down to Walgren, if Mr. Sharp wanted the bill to pass. So we were protected in any event.

CHAPTER SIXTY

ADJOURNMENT "SINE DIE"

APRIL 23, 9:30 A.M. -- THE FULL coalition was meeting in Freeport's conference room for the debriefing. Bob Cole began by giving voice to the thought that had absorbed me ever since the 21-20 vote in full committee. "Tauzin's decision not to push Texaco's position may well have been the last straw for them. Sure, we need to stay alert, but I suspect this thing is over."

"Well, that's sure a hopeful note to start this meeting on," said King. "Anyone have any information that might lead us to a different view?"

Rosemary spoke up, "I've checked with Dave Finnegan, Dingell's man, about when Speaker O'Neill might allow the bill to go to the Rules Committee. Finnegan said it's way too early to even think about that. So with no action yet on the horizon on the Senate floor, I guess I agree with Bob, even though the bill has gone through the committee level in both houses."

Foster added, "That's true, Rosemary, and I'd say it's because the overall legislation is still hellaciously complex and controversial. I think the leadership in both houses, Majority Leader Baker and Speaker O'Neill, don't want to bring this thing to the floor and see other legislation get derailed while natural gas decontrol ties the Congress in knots."

When King searched the room for other views, there were none, and we adjourned "sine die," as they say in Congress. Things had finally come to at least a temporary halt, and so far, we had won.

EPILOGUE

THE HOUSE Energy and Commerce Committee report contained nothing to endanger our victories in that committee.

There were occasional false alarms through the rest of 1984 -- rumors that the bill was being readied for Senate floor action or for the House Rules Committee -- but they proved to be just rumors.

In 1985, the Reagan Administration made it clear that they still wanted to decontrol natural gas prices. Bill Foster and the First Four went back to the Department of Energy and met again with Deputy Secretary Danny Boggs, who assured us that the president and the administration wanted a new, clean bill, one that sharply limited the number of contentious issues.

I raised the obvious question: "So, does that mean you won't include the language we opposed, in the new bill?"

"Yes, it does," came the reply, as Bill Foster nodded and the First Four breathed a collective sigh of relief. Our long battle was finally over.

* * *

The natural gas decontrol bill finally did pass, in 1986, with no mention of renegotiating first-sale, not-for-resale intrastate gas. Our coalition's companies were protected. The overall scheme of price decontrol has continued to this day.

PPG went on to maintain good relations with Senator Heinz, and

I worked closely with Heinz and members of his staff other than Tenet, on two environmental issues in the next several years, before the senator was tragically killed in the crash of a light plane trying to land in Pittsburgh. I attended his packed memorial service at the National Cathedral in Washington.

Senator Henry "Scoop" Jackson passed away on September 1, 1983, never having returned to an active role in the Senate. His seat was taken, the same day, by the state's former Republican governor, Dan Evans. Several of the House members mentioned in the story went on to win seats in the U.S. Senate; some of them are still there.

The final tab for Patton, Boggs and Blow came to just under a quarter of a million dollars, or about sixty-two thousand to PPG, some thirteen thousand less than I had estimated to Bill Harris. Bob Cole was able to convince his management to meet their full share after they had reached their thirty thousand dollar cap.

Cole, Lew Dale, John Ferguson and I remained close, with two or more of us occasionally playing tennis or going out for an evening with our wives. Russell King joined us a couple of times for tennis. We all knew this had been what I came to call a "career case," a battle that was long, hard and tense, but one that we were ultimately glad had included us.

MEMBERS OF THE SENATE ENERGY AND NATURAL RESOURCES COMMITTEE 103RD CONGRESS, 1983-84

James McClure (R-ID) – Chairman
Bennett Johnston (D-LA) – Ranking Democrat
Lloyd Bentsen (D-TX)
Bill Bradley (D-NJ)
Dale Bumpers (D-AK)
Thad Cochran (R-MS)
Pete Domenici (R-NM)
Wendell Ford (D-KY)
Mark Hatfield (R-OR)
John Heinz (R-PA)
Henry Jackson (D-WA)*
Carl Levin (D-MI)
Spark Matsunaga (D-HI)
John Melcher (R-MT)
Howard Metzenbaum (D-OH)
Frank Murkowski (R-AK)
Don Nickles (R-OK)
Sam Nunn (D-GA)
Ted Stevens (R-AK)
Malcolm Wallop (R-WY)
John Warner (R-VA)
Lowell Weicker (R-CT)

*Died September 1, 1983; replaced by Dan Evans (R-WA)

MEMBERS OF THE HOUSE ENERGY AND COMMERCE COMMITTEE 103ʳᴰ CONGRESS, 1983-84

John Dingell (D-MI), Chairman
Ralph Hall (R-TX), Ranking Republican
Tom Bliley (R-VA)
Jim Broyhill (R-NC)
John Bryant (R-TX)
Jim Coats (R-IN)
Cardiss Collins (D-IL)
Tom Corcoran (R-IL)
Bill Dannemeyer (R-CA)
Norman Dix (D-WA)
Wayne Dowdy (D-MS)
Bob Eckhardt (R-TX)
Jack Fields (R-TX)
Jim Florio (D-NJ)
Al Gore (D-TN)
Mickey Leland (D-TX)
Norm Lent (R-NY)
Tom Luken (D-OH)
Ed Madigan (R-IL)
Ed Markey (D-MA)
Barbara Mikulski (D-MD)
Carlos Moorhead (R-CA)
Howard Nielsen (R-UT)
Jim Oberstar (D-MN)
Dick Ottinger (D-NY)
Mike Oxley (R-OH)
Bill Richardson (D-NM)
Matt Rinaldo (R-NJ)
Don Ritter (R-PA)
Paul Rogers (D-FL)
Jim Scheuer (D-NY)
Phil Sharp (D-IN)
Richard Shelby (D-AL)
Gerry Sikorski (D-MN)
Jim Slattery (R-KS)
Al Swift (D-WA)
Mike Synar (D-OK)
Billy Tauzin (D-LA)
Doug Walgren (D-PA)
Henry Waxman (D-CA)
Tim Wirth (D-CO)
Ron Wyden (D-OR)